Laurens Hedegaard is a spiritual teacher and a therapist as well. He has been teaching seminars and workshops for 15 years, teaching his students clairvoyance and Reiki healing with their own personal development as the primary goal. Laurens enjoys mountain biking and travelling. Putting the two together is the ultimate combination.

Pernille Sorensen works as both an energy healer and therapist. She discovered her abilities as a medium almost 15 years ago. She has published four children's books for 4-8-year olds. They are all a part of her *Dappa & Nappa* series that focus on a child's inner life and feelings. Some hobbies of hers include travelling and watching her local ice hockey team play.

Laurens and Pernille met in 2003 and were married in 2013. The couple is currently residing near Copenhagen, Denmark. Teaming up together, they help the living and deceased better understand the afterlife and themselves.

Laurens Hedegaard and Pernille Sorensen

CONVERSATIONS WITH GHOSTS

AUSTIN MACAULEY PUBLISHERS™

LONDON • CAMBRIDGE • NEW YORK • SHARJAH

A CIP catalogue record for this title is available from the British Library.

ISBN 9781398444379 (Paperback)
ISBN 9781398444386 (Hardback)
ISBN 9781398444409 (ePub e-book)
ISBN 9781398444393 (Audiobook)

www.austinmacauley.com

First Published 2023
Austin Macauley Publishers Ltd®
1 Canada Square
Canary Wharf
London
E14 5AA

This book has been on its way for more than a decade and different people have helped us along the way.

First and foremost, we wish to thank all the families who asked for our help and invited us into their homes, and thereby made it possible for us to get in touch with these spirits who needed a helping hand to cross over. We feel very privileged and honoured to be able to help you, as well as the spirits, find peace or acceptance and move on in a new direction.

To Heidi Korsgaard from Skriveværkstedet. Thank you for your positive feedback and support in the initial process and for helping us shape this book.

To Anja Duna, our transcriptionist extraordinaire. You made our lives a whole lot easier. Thank you for your positive feedback every time we sent you a new interview.

Many thanks to everyone who has supported our work and who continues to recommend us to other people even years after we last saw you.

A big thank you to Austin Macauley Publishers for believing in this book and for giving us the opportunity to publish.

A special thank you to our family and friends who have accepted our unusual path. We know our work can seem a bit strange, and so can we.

A very special thanks to Kristen Cook who has read and re-read every page and helped us get it right. You're the best and we are so appreciative of all your help.

Last, but certainly not least, thank you to 'The Club of the Wise Masters.' You mean the world to us and you make us seem far wiser than we are.

Table of Contents

Ghost, Spirits, Phantoms

*They go by many names, but we've chosen to call them
ghosts*

*As a general rule, ghosts are neither evil nor out to scare us;
they are lost and terrified souls
that desperately need attention
and a chance to tell their story.
If they get to share their message, it makes sense to them
that they've had to live a life of great sorrow.
Then they can finally escape their captivity between death
and the afterlife.*

Preface

Ghosts Have Messages for Us

Ghosts rarely wish to hurt or scare us. More often than not, they're lost souls carrying the burden of heavy emotional baggage. They need our help to release this baggage – only then can they move on from this place and escape the limbo between death and the afterlife.

Over the past couple of years, we've communicated with a series of ghosts in both private homes and office spaces. This book recounts ten conversations that we've had with ghosts. Each story is unique, and they all unfold at different times. What the ghosts had in common was that they all had a message they wanted to share – and the places and people they chose to approach in an attempt to fulfil that mission were never random. Ghosts usually have a connection to the house or building they wind up staying in or, wanting that, they feel like they have something in common with one of the residents. Those are the main reasons they end up where they end up.

Whenever we talk to ghosts and work towards helping them cross over, the process usually goes something like this: we visit the home that the ghost is living in, and we have a conversation with the ghost that lasts two to three hours.

Before we establish contact with the ghost, we talk to the residents. The people living in the house can't hear the ghost, but Pernille can. She hears what the ghost is saying and relays its voice. She talks at the same pace and in the same tone of voice as the ghost, and she uses the same words. Laurens asks the questions. The common denominator for these conversations is that they provide a sense of resolution for something that the resident is hiding or struggling with.

Some of the people we visit are sceptical at the beginning, but their attitudes change over the course of our visit – or afterwards, when they find documents, such as pictures in a local archive, that verify the authenticity of the ghost's story. Many people are touched by the conversations and cry while the ghost talks because someone has come along and put their everyday challenges – or the overarching themes of their lives – into words. Others shed a few tears because they meet someone who has truly struggled, only to witness them finding peace and being reunited with their loved ones at the end of the conversation, as they finally move on to the afterlife.

Ghosts are just as different as the people we visit. Some want to talk to us and are relieved to find that we can hear them, whereas others are more withdrawn, if not reluctant. A ghost's reluctancy often stems from unfinished emotional challenges and situations, such as anxiety, grief, confusion, low self-esteem, and similar feelings of inadequacy that they have brought with them from their time on this earth. Our conversations with the ghosts are all about working through these feelings to give them a smooth transition into the afterlife. Once the ghosts have told us their story, they're usually willing to say goodbye to this life and move on for good.

This book is written in dialogue to mimic the way these conversations play out. Our hope is that this will make it easier for you to imagine the flow of the conversations. Names and places, as well as descriptions of the family members living in the haunted residence, have been changed to ensure anonymity – but the conversations are real. We hope they can give you an insight into the world that most of us cannot see but that all of us can learn from.

Before we get started on the actual conversations, we want to talk to you about how we first began to start talking to ghosts.

Happy reading.
Pernille and Laurens

The Story That Started It All
The Ghost at the Institution

Laurens' Story

Some years ago, I was in a place where I needed change. I'd been working in the moving industry for almost 20 years and decided to try something completely different. I landed a job as a helper at an institution for people with multiple disabilities. There were nine residents at the institution, all of whom had severe mental and physical disabilities and had no language or other means of communicating aside from expressions, sounds and incomprehensible gestures.

In my department, there was a girl named Tanja. She screamed a lot, and she flung herself from side to side so much that she slept in a bed built like an aquarium. Nobody had ever considered the possibility that there might be a specific reason for her restlessness. As far as the others were concerned, she had mental and physical disabilities and reacting in this way was just part of her disability.

I'd been working at the institution for a while when I had my first solo nightshift. Night after night, I heard Tanja scream, but in the beginning, I didn't pay much attention – after all, the others had said that that was just what she was like and what she had always been like. As time went on, I began to pick up on differences in her screaming. One night, she was screaming particularly loudly, and I went into her room, only to be greeted by a chill that made my hairs stand on end. Her radiator was cold, but when I walked over to turn it on, I discovered that it was already turned on. It just wasn't heating up. I didn't really think about it, but I did make a note of the fact that her radiator wasn't working to make sure that someone would come fix it.

This chain of events began to repeat itself after that. Every time I walked into her room, it was cold, and her radiator still appeared to be broken. I spent a lot of time complaining about that – surely, it couldn't be that difficult to get an HVAC contractor out to solve the problem?

One night, I was on another solo nightshift, and I heard the most heart-breaking scream, and I ran towards her room. Just as I was about to walk in, a smell that I didn't recognise hit my nose. It smelled simultaneously damp and burned. I opened the door to her room, where I was once again met with bitter cold even though her windows were closed and the radiator was turned all the way up. I tried to calm her down but sensed that there was something in the room. I couldn't see it, but it felt pretty terrifying. I sat with the girl and managed to calm her down, and little by little, the room began to heat back up. When I left the room and found myself back out in the hallway, the smell returned, and I walked around to see if it was coming from old laundry or something like that, but I couldn't find anything.

Some time passed, and then the heart-breaking scream, the smell, and the cold returned to the room. I was on a shift with two of my colleagues, when Tanja started screaming again. I asked my colleagues to listen and asked them if they could hear the differences in her screaming. We listened for a short while, and then they said that the screams were heart-breaking, and they shuddered. I went on to tell them about my experiences with the smell, cold, and the radiator. The story put them on edge, but I asked them to walk down to the girl with me.

"Do you recognise that smell?" I asked my colleagues when we were standing outside her door.

"I think it's sulphur," one of them answered.

"Whenever this smell is here, it's cold in Tanja's room – even if her radiator is turned all the way up and the windows are closed."

We walked into the room, and my colleagues felt all the things I'd told them about. One of them turned around and walked back out of the room while the other stood rooted to the spot, as if frozen in place. I tried to speak to him, but his speech was incomprehensible, and he seemed to be in a state of shock. I managed to get him out of the room and close the door, leaving me alone with the girl who was still screaming. Then I pulled up a chair and asked the presence that I sensed in the room to have a seat. I pulled up another chair and sat down. I closed my eyes, took a deep breath, and let go of all thoughts and theories as to what the presence could be. All of a sudden, the room was calm, and I sensed that there was a girl sitting on the chair across from me. She was between 12 and 14 years old, and she was scared.

"Why are you here? What do you want with the girl in this room?" I asked her.

She told me that she'd perished in a terrible fire, unable to escape, and when the fire had been put out, her body was burned beyond all recognition. She couldn't find anyone who could tell her what to do or where to go.

"How long have you been here?" I asked.

"I don't know, but it's probably been a couple of years," she answered.

Her story touched me, and as she told her story, I listened so intently that it painted one mental image after the other. I felt her anxiety, loneliness, and feelings of powerlessness and despair, and the tears flowed down my cheeks. I thought I must be able to help her move on to wherever she was going.

All of a sudden, light came pouring in through the ceiling as if rays of sunlight were bursting through the roof and into the room. The girl on the chair looked at me with fear, and to my surprise, I told her, as if it was the most natural thing in the world that someone had come to find her. In that moment, it was like someone reached down to grab her with two big hands and lifted her up as if she were a baby bird. Calm, protecting, and compassionate.

"Don't be afraid – just go with them," I told her.

Right before she disappeared, she flashed me a smile that pulled at my heartstrings and made my tears begin to flow anew.

I stayed seated for a while to recover while the room returned to its normal state. Tanja was calm, and she was practically smiling and chuckling while the heat returned to her room. I walked back out and discovered that the smell was gone. Everything was back to normal. I went back to my colleagues. I told them what had happened just to hear it out loud. They had a hard time wrapping their heads around it all, but I could feel that the events had sparked something within me.

The experience told me that this was something I could do. I could help souls that were trapped between death and the afterlife for whatever reason, and the events of that night also turned out to help Tanja who stopped her particularly heart-breaking screaming. It was the first time I had contact with a ghost, and I thought it felt pretty natural. I was very surprised at the way I handled it. All of a sudden, something vague became concrete, and something unknown became known. And it helped both parties.

That night paved the way for more conversations with ghosts.

Chapter 1
Flemming's Double Life
Stand by Who You Are

Ghita is in her early 40s and lives in a three-bedroom apartment in Copenhagen. For months, she's had the feeling that someone is watching her. She hears strange sounds in her apartment, from one of the rooms in particular. When she stays in the room for longer periods of time, she tends to get a headache or become unusually tired. Now she's reached out to us for help. A ghost appears in the apartment and tells us about his secret double life and not having the courage to live the life he dreamed of.

Pernille and Laurens haven't been in Ghita's apartment for long before they sense the presence of a male ghost. The ghost seems a little reserved, but they still get the impression that he would like to communicate.

"Can you tell me your name?" Laurens asks.

"You're here to make fun of me," the ghost answers.

"Of course not, we're here to hear what you have to say. We think you might have something important to tell Ghita."

"Okay…My name is Flemming."

"How old are you, Flemming?"

"Forty-six."

"How long have you been living here?"

"A couple of months, I think."

"Why did you move in? And how did you get here?"

"Hmm...I followed Ghita home. She passed me in the street, and I could feel that she was kind of like me. I've been lonely for so long, I thought I'd go with her. She might be able to understand me."

"In what way do you think she's like you?"

"She also feels different, and she's leading a double life, just like me."

"What do you mean by a double life?"

"I mean that Ghita acts like one person at work, but inside, she's someone else, and she only shows that side of her to a few people, if any."

Pernille and Laurens look over at Ghita who doesn't say anything but offers an affirmative nod.

"She's scared that she won't be respected at work if she shows her true colours. I've always had the same fear," Flemming says.

"Do you want to tell me a little more about your double life?"

Flemming hesitates.

"Yes, but it's hard to talk about it without sounding stupid." He takes a break before he continues, "I've always been very focused on my career. I've done well for myself and earned a lot of money. I was in a management position for many years, with great responsibility and a lot of people beneath me. I usually wear a suit and look like any other businessman in the industry." Flemming takes another break.

"Now, don't misunderstand me. I've always liked women…but ever since I was a teenager, I've had this desire…bordering on craving to wear beautiful clothes…um, women's clothes…" Flemming looks at Laurens and Pernille, waiting for their response.

"You can continue if you want to. I'd love to hear your story," Laurens says.

"Well…I love the feeling of silk against my skin. I've always struggled to accept that part of myself. But this one time, I bought some beautiful dresses. I only wore them when I was alone…behind closed curtains, of course. It seems so strange, and I'm sure that my employees would have had a very hard time taking me seriously if they'd known about this part of me." Flemming sighs deeply. "Phew, there it is. That's my secret."

"Have you never told anyone else? A close friend or family member?" Laurens asks.

"No. I lived two separate lives. I was a career person who had things under control, but I also had this part of me that I didn't want to show to anyone. I couldn't figure out how it could fit into my life. I was scared that it would damage the respect and recognition I had," Flemming answers.

The Lure of Female Beauty

"Do you want to tell us a little about your upbringing?"

"Hmm, I guess I can do that. It's actually nice to finally talk to someone. I'm from a classic nuclear family consisting of a mom, dad, and two kids. I'm the youngest, and my sister is four years older than me."

"What did your dad do for a living?"

"He was a blacksmith, and he was what you would call a broad-shouldered man."

"Someone who commanded respect?"

"He was a masculine man in the way that a lot of tradesmen are. You know, someone with big old blacksmith's mitts," Flemming answers with a chuckle.

"When did you grow up?"

"In the 1940s."

"What did your mom do for a living?"

"She was a receptionist."

"So, you grew up in the 40s. Did you go to school?"

"Yes. I was good at the academic stuff, and my teachers described me as a sharp boy."

"What was your housing situation like?"

"We lived in a small house with a kitchen and living room downstairs and three bedrooms upstairs, my parents' bedroom and mine and my sister's. I had the room right next to my sister."

As Flemming tells his story, Pernille receives a mental image of Flemming's older sister having friends over. She has closed the door to her room, but Flemming is standing outside and peeping in through the keyhole. The girls are doing each other's hair, and they're trying on each other's dresses.

"I'm incredibly fascinated by them. I almost feel drawn to what they're doing, and I find it hard to let go," Flemming elaborates.

"How old are you at this point?"

"Around 12 or 13. That's when I really start to find girls interesting."

"Go on. 'Interesting' in what way?"

"Both in the girlfriend way and because of the beauty."

21

"The beauty?"

"Yes, they love beautiful, exquisite things, but that's not something I see in my own surroundings. That said, my dad was quick to accept that I wasn't good with my hands."

"That you weren't cut out for the life of a blacksmith?"

"Yes. My teachers told him that I was an intelligent boy, and that I should put my skills to good use in the business world. So, I end up training to be a banker. Aside from the fact that I liked numbers, the thing that appealed to me was that I had to dress nice every day. Polish my shoes, put on a suit, and wear a tie. Make an effort. I like that a lot."

"So, you remember your childhood as peaceful, calm, and completely ordinary?" Laurens asks.

"I wouldn't say it was ordinary because it didn't take me long to pick up on the fact that my friends and dad thought there was a clear separation between men and women. There were men's things and issues, and then there were women's things and issues, but I never told them that I thought the women's things were beautiful. The women themselves...well, we could all agree on that" – Flemming laughs – "but I got the impression that I was the only one attracted by the beauty in a way that made me want to try it out on my own body."

"What was the relationship between your mom and dad like?"

"I'd describe it as harmonic. The only chaos was inside me. I didn't ever tell them about that. I didn't want to flip their worlds upside-down by confiding in them. You know, just come right out and say, 'Dad, I want to try on my sister's dresses.' I was completely up to date on what was appropriate and what wasn't, and my mom and dad had high hopes for me because I had the chance to build a career without destroying myself physically the way my dad did.

"But the banking world is also a conservative one, all about reputation, decency, and – of course – who you know. You worked your way up through other people's recommendations, so I never dared reveal this part of me out of fear that everyone would find out that I was attracted to women's clothes. If that happened, it would mean the end of my career. And it was the only one I had. All my opportunities were within finance – I wouldn't be able to fend for myself in my dad's world. I can't even hammer a nail properly. I mean, I can get it in, but I can't guarantee that it'll look nice," Flemming says with a laugh. "I repressed that part of me, which meant that I was never truly happy. I rose through the ranks and did well for myself, but I struggled to be happy on the inside because I felt like I was repressing my true colours."

The Girlfriends of Adolescence

"How old are you when you met your first girlfriend?"

"Depends how you define 'girlfriend'."

"A relationship with a woman."

"I slow-danced with a girl when I was 12 years old. Her name was Henriette. We were at a dance, and she kissed me on the cheek, so I fell head over heels. I held her hands sometimes. Things were very different back then. Relationships were nothing like they are today. It took a long time before anyone dared to do anything. But Henriette was my first kiss."

"Did you ever get into a real relationship? A sexual one, I mean?"

"Of course, I started a relationship with Lise when I was 17 years old."

"I get the feeling that you're a handsome man?"

"Why, thank you. Many would consider me a stylish man. I made an effort, but that was perfectly acceptable within my line of work. My clothes were always impeccably ironed. That wouldn't have worked in my dad's field." Flemming smiles.

"When did you meet Lise?"

"She became a fellow trainee at the bank. She was going to be a secretary, and I was going to be a banker."

"I just thought of something. Where did you grow up?"

"Up north, in Hjørring."

"Okay. I wanted to get an idea of where all of this is unfolding. What was your relationship with Lise like? How did you feel? Did you find it difficult?"

"Well, feelings are never simple when you're 17, are they" – Flemming laughs – "but she was sweet and beautiful and had a calm personality, and I like that. My parents called her a well-behaved girl. She liked art and beautiful things, and that suited me perfectly."

"So, you had mutual interests?"

"Yes, I remember it as uncomplicated. I remember the paradox of everything seeming uncomplicated on the outside, with loving parents, a loving girlfriend, and a career around the corner, and then having this secret to nag me."

"How long were you and Lise together?"

"Many years. We get married and have kids. There was a year where we almost didn't see each other because I finished my training and moved to Copenhagen. I was offered a position as a junior advisor in the capital, and she stayed in

Hjørring to finish her own training. Then we got married, and she moved to Copenhagen to be with me. So, there wasn't a lot of drama in my life, and things went smoother than they did for other people. My only problems were internal. I felt like I was lying – that I wasn't being true to myself. I had a hard time coping with the fact that I wanted to wear dresses. It wasn't because I wanted to be with other men, and it wasn't because I felt like a woman. I felt like a man, but I thought there was something fantastically beautiful about being dressed like a woman, and I didn't associate it with something that made me question my sexuality."

"You married Lise. How many kids did you have?"

"We had two kids, two boys."

"How did you feel about becoming a dad?"

"It was big. It was an amazing feeling, and I was fine with the responsibility."

"How old were you when you had your first kid?"

"I became a father pretty late; I was 24. Lise is two years younger than me, so she was 22 at the time."

"So, your family was blessed with the arrival of a son when you were 24?"

"Yes, and the second arrived a year later. The only thing that nagged me was the fact that I struggled to be happy even though everything around me was uncomplicated and…It was almost like I was missing the pure feeling. Do you know what I mean?" Flemming asks.

"I know what you mean," Laurens answers.

"You look around, but it's like the last piece is missing."

"Yeah, I understand what you're saying. I experienced something similar a few years ago. Everyone around me was saying that I had everything, but inside, something was

25

closing in on me, making me want to create changes while also making me anxious," Laurens says.

"Exactly, it was like I was missing myself. I didn't have anywhere that I could be me. I had to keep up appearances both at home and in public. That made it hard for me to enjoy it. I had a wonderful wife and two amazing kids, but I didn't have myself." Flemming takes a break.

"Yeah," Laurens says.

"And that made things difficult."

"I understand that. If you can't be yourself, everything else has a tendency to feel pointless. It can stop you from being part of your own life. Almost like you're on the outside looking in."

"That's right."

"But the years pass, Flemming. How are things with the family and at work for the next four to five years?"

"Things are outwardly great, but the feeling of emptiness grows. I start seeking out a place where I can be myself."

"A community?"

"Yes, a community, but I can't find one. There are homosexual communities, but I'm not homosexual, so I didn't feel like I fit in. I'm a crossdresser. I'm sure of my sexuality, but sometimes, I want the other side. Not all the time, just once in a while. Just like you might want to go out and play cards or pool every Wednesday. I needed to let it out occasionally, but I couldn't find anywhere to do that."

The Apartment

"Then what do you do?" Laurens asks.

26

"I rent a one-bedroom apartment and go there once a week. I tell Lise that I have a meeting to attend."

"Are you still working in the bank at this point?"

"No, I've become an accountant for a big accounting firm, and I have multiple people working under me, but the frustration inside me is still going strong. So, I rent this small one-bedroom apartment and draw the curtains so nobody can see me through the windows when I dress in women's clothes. Then I stand in front of the mirror and admire myself," Flemming says with a smile in his voice. "After a while, I've lived out that part of me, and I put my suit back on and go home to my family."

"How do you feel when you look at yourself in the mirror? What happens inside you?"

Flemming is quiet for a little while before answering.

"I become whole. It's an amazing feeling." Flemming pauses shortly. "I don't need a community. I just need permission to do this. It's not about wanting to cheat on my wife…I can't explain it. It's almost like I have this urge, and that this weekly rendezvous with myself, well, makes me complete."

"A meeting with who you are deep down?"

"Yes, that's what it feels like." Flemming sounds relieved that his feelings are being understood.

"It's a wonderful feeling to find the thing that makes you complete, whatever that might be. For how long did you rent the apartment?"

"Fourteen years."

"So, you're in your late 30s?"

"I'm in my early 40s."

"How are things with your boys around then?"

"Good. They're both intelligent, doing well in school, and good at numbers, but they have a sporty side that I've never had, and they play a lot of football. As the years go by, my wife begins to struggle more and more. She's worried that I'm seeing another woman."

"So, she can feel that something is wrong?"

"Yes, she's curious about all these meetings of mine. One night, the youngest gets sick, so she tries to call me at work, but nobody picks up because everyone has gone home."

"Then what happens?"

"It's a big dilemma for me…should I reveal my secret…and face her disgust, or risk her leaving me because she thinks I'm unfaithful?"

"That must be a difficult dilemma to find yourself in."

"Very much so."

"What do you decide?"

"I decide that I'm not brave enough to tell her the truth."

"What are the consequences of that decision?"

"She asks me if I'm being unfaithful, and I say no because I'm not. She sets me an ultimatum and says that I need to cut out the weekly meeting, but I tell her that I can't because it's part of my job. We leave the discussion alone for a couple of weeks, but one day, she follows me. She watches me walk into the small apartment…And as soon as I've gone upstairs, she knocks on the door, and I'm forced to open it."

"Have you had the chance to change?"

"No, I'm still wearing my suit, but there's a long dress on a hanger on the mirror, and she sees that when she opens the door."

"What happens then?"

"When she notices the dress, she turns around and leaves…and I don't try to follow her…I stay in the apartment."

"Oh, wow…"

"That's how I felt too."

"How did you feel in that situation?"

"I'm disappointed with myself…that I'm not brave enough to be vulnerable and show her who I truly am…It could've made a massive difference in our marriage…Apparently, I'm not a brave man." Flemming sighs deeply.

"But there are a lot of issues that have been going on for a little too long. And the longer we let things go on, the harder it can be to get back out."

"Exactly. I felt trapped…by the time, as well. It's like things are different in your time. There are many different types of people, and although one group might not accept the other, there are more people in each group – or they're more visible, at least – so you don't feel so alone. I'm sure there were other people like me in my time, but I couldn't find anyone. Or rather, I didn't know where to look."

"Yeah, these days you can communicate with people from all over the world, and with chatrooms and social media, you're bound to find someone who feels the same way that you do," Laurens explains.

"I was scared that I would be despised if I showed my true colours to anyone. I didn't read or hear about it, so even though it was harmless, it felt dangerous."

"You were scared of being cast out?"

"Worst-case scenario, yes. That was my fear. When she walks away from me at the apartment, she tells me not to come home, so I don't."

"So, you never go home again?"

"Only to pick up some of my things."

"How old are the boys at this point?"

"16 and 17."

"Do you talk to them?"

"I call them, but they're very mad at me because they think I've chosen another woman over them and their mom. When I talk to Lise, she gives me plenty of opportunities to explain myself, but I don't have the courage to tell her the truth." Flemming's voice is overflowing with sadness. "I'm scared of the judgement of society. In those days, it's more acceptable to cheat on your wife than to be someone who wants to wear women's clothes. So, I moved into the one-bedroom apartment permanently."

God's Punishment

"How are things at work after you move out of the family home?"

"People are understanding because everyone thinks our marriage ended because I found someone else. And I don't correct them. I'm not necessarily met with excitement, but more of an attitude of 'oh, well, it happens', and seeing as I have such a good reputation at work, nobody blames me."

"It's a strange time for me because I'm grieving the loss of my family. My kids are so mad at me that they don't want to see me, but still, I go through a period of happiness because I have this ritual of coming home from work, drawing the

30

curtains, and changing. This is a period in my life where I feel more connected to myself than ever before, and where I 'am' myself for hours at a time and not just for short bursts of time like I was used to. But it was a strange dilemma. Before, I had a life that seemed happy on the outside but felt empty on the inside, where I only experienced a feeling of complete comfort for short bursts of time. Now, I'm heartbroken because I've lost my family, but at the same time, I feel ecstatic because I get to be myself."

"The conflict has shifted?"

"Yes, it's almost like I can't have it all. When I'm here" – Flemming gestures to the room – "I'm missing this, and when I'm there, I'm missing the other thing."

"The way you see it, do you have to commit to one of the two and then leave the other behind, or where do you stand?"

"I think I had to be brave enough to embrace all of it and see where it took me. But I didn't have the courage."

"What happens as time goes on?" Laurens asks.

"Well, around three quarters of a year later, I get a lung infection, and I have an awful cough for a long time."

"Do you ever wonder whether your lung infection might have something to do with the fact that you were under pressure for such a long time or that you might be worn out?"

"Actually, I find myself wondering if it could be God's punishment," Flemming chuckles uncertainly and continues, "for not being honest and for being who I am."

"Does the lung infection spell the end for you?"

"Well…I guess you could say that, but probably not the way you think. One day, I get a coughing fit as I'm biking home from work. I start swerving so much that I crash and hit my head on the concrete. So, it was an accident, but it was the direct result of my lung infection."

Shocking Encounter Provides Resolution

"When do you realise that you're dead?"

"When I see my mom who had died the year before."

"So, she came to pick you up?"

"Yes."

"But you didn't go with her?"

"No, I'm too ashamed. I know how important the nuclear family is to her, and I've destroyed my own family with this silly idea of mine. So, I tell her that I need more time and that she should just go…ahead. I'm not ready yet. I need some time to lick my wounds."

"You felt like there's something you need to do first?"

"Exactly, there's something I needed to sort out. She understands and leaves."

"What did you do in the time that follows?"

"I wander the streets and spend a lot of time looking back on my life. One day, I bump into Ghita, and I can see that she's walking around with the same empty feeling. On the outside, it looks like she has things under control, but on the inside, something is missing. She doesn't feel like herself." Flemming takes a break. "So, I think…once upon a time finding like-minded people was important to me, and maybe she feels the same way. I thought that we could keep each other company if I followed her, and so I went with her."

"So, you never told anyone about your desire to wear dresses? You never got that off your chest?"

"Hmm…that day when I was peeping on my sister and her friends through the keyhole, they suddenly opened the door, and my sister said: 'What, are you standing here watching us?' And I dared to ask if I could join in." Flemming pauses and continues, "And then they all scream with laughter and mock me. And that's when I promise myself never to let that happen ever again. I don't want to be ridiculed." Flemming falls silent again.

"So, you put a lid on your feelings and bravery, Flemming? I can feel that someone has arrived. Someone who wants to show themselves to you and tell you something…Hold on, I'll step aside."

Flemming reacts with a mixture of shock and excitement when he notices the figure that appears in the apartment. It's Lise. She steps forward and smiles at him, as she says: "You're such a fool of a man, Flemming. How on earth could you think that I wouldn't accept it?"

"Well, I just couldn't imagine you wanting to be with a man like that," Flemming said, his voice still betraying his surprise.

Lise chuckles and continues.

"It might have surprised me, but I would have been able to live with it. It's a small price to pay for everything we had and could've had, don't you think?"

Flemming walks over to Lise.

"I'm just so embarrassed…I-I don't really know what to say."

"I just wish you had been braver," Lise says, the smile still on her face.

Laurens speaks to her.

"Lise, can I ask how long you've been dead?"

"Of course. I died recently, and when I discovered that Flemming hadn't left yet, I thought that I should probably go get him myself. Otherwise, he'll never move on." She laughs lovingly and looks at Flemming.

"Aren't you mad at me?" Flemming asks.

"Flemming, don't you remember our deal?" Lise smiles and looks at him intently. "Together, we agreed that this life was all about you finding the courage." She laughs again.

Flemming holds his hand to his forehead.

"You're right, I remember now. Courage could have changed my life, but I was scared of being judged by society and my surroundings. My life's purpose was to be brave and dare to stand by who I am. But I was only brave enough to do that in secret."

"In your time as a ghost or a soul on earth, did you ever visit your boys?"

"Yes, and I've seen how much baggage I've left them with. They both have a weakness that stems from being abandoned by their dad as teenagers. Both have gone on to be successful, but they never feel like they're good enough, which is something they have to work through. They want to feel whole again. They don't know that that's what they're looking for yet, but I hope they both find it."

"I don't think you spend your time wondering if the other path would have been better if you feel whole. I think you focus on where you are because that feels good and right," Laurens says.

"I think you might be right about that."

"In hindsight, I can see that I could've gained a lot from showing people who I really was, but I wasn't brave enough to try."

"I'm sure you'll get another chance," Laurens says with a smile.

"I'm sure of that too," Flemming answers.

"Then I hope that things work out for you. Is there anything else you would like to share?" Laurens asks.

"I'd just like to tell Ghita something: Follow your heart because you can't be happy if you don't feel complete. If you feel whole inside, you can handle even more on the outside. It's important to feel good about yourself, otherwise you can't show other people how you feel."

"We should get going," Lise says and extends her hand.

"Yes," Flemming says, turning to face Ghita one last time. "I hope you find your courage and that things work out for you."

A sudden burst of light appears in the form of a staircase. They ascend and slowly fade out.

Laurens turns to look at Ghita.

"How do you feel?"

"I'm very tired, but I feel fine. Flemming's story has given me insight that I didn't have before. I can feel that I need to do something about my situation, but before that, I need to relax."

Chapter 2
Klara's Forbidden Love
Trust Can Change Everything

Ever since Charlotte moved into her house with her two young kids three years ago, she has had the feeling that someone or something was in the house. It hasn't scared her, but when her four-year-old son saw a woman's figure and started to describe her as 'the girl sitting in the living room', she decided to investigate. The ghost that appears tells us a brutal story about the fatal consequences of not sharing our problems with other people.

One evening, Pernille and Laurens journeyed to Charlotte's house north of Copenhagen. The house is surrounded by fields and the closest neighbours are about 300 feet away. Charlotte has arranged for someone to take care of the kids to give the adults a chance to investigate the house. Pernille and Laurens start out by walking around the house to get a feel for it and to pick up on the energies of the different rooms. It doesn't take them long to pick up on a female presence and realise that something is following them out of curiosity. Pernille, Laurens, and Charlotte sit down in the living room.

"This is where I usually sense something, especially when I'm relaxing and watching TV. It's like someone wants something from me," Charlotte explains. "This is also where my youngest son has seen the female figure."

As Pernille, Laurens, and Charlotte sit on the couch, Pernille sees an image of a ghost. A young woman with long, blonde hair sits down in one of the armchairs across from the couch.

"Hello, can I ask what your name is?" Laurens looks at the armchair.

"I'm Klara," the ghost answers, looking shyly down at her hands.

"How old are you, Klara?"

"16."

"Have you been here long?"

"Yes," Klara answers with a nod.

"Where are you from and where did you grow up."

"Near the coast, not too far from Elsinore."

"Which decade are we talking about?"

"I was a teenager in the post-war years."

"The First or Second World War?"

"The Second, of course. I was a child during the war, and I was a teenager in the 50s."

Laurens chuckles and continues.

"Of course, it was the Second World War. Can you tell me a little about your family situation?"

"I lived on a small farm in the countryside with my parents and two younger siblings."

"How much older are you?"

"Six and seven years respectively."

"How were things at school?"

"Things were good. I was described as a well-behaved girl, and I got recognition for being hard-working. After school, I helped my mom watch the kids. My mom watched my younger siblings and a few of the neighbours' kids."

"What did your dad do?"

"He used to be a farmer, but after the war, he started working in a factory."

"Did he come home every day?"

"Of course."

"Did your mom do anything besides watching the kids?"

"Yes, she cooked and brought food to some of the elderly people in town. I've always considered her a thoughtful person with her heart in the right place."

"What was your relationship with your mom like?"

"We were very close, and we trusted each other. My mom was very proud of me. She always told me that I had many opportunities and that the world would need women like me and that my generation would be presented with more opportunities than hers. My mom was a smart woman. She told me that things would change after the war, and that more and more women would start to join the workforce. That was why it was important to do well in school, so I could take advantage of the opportunities I would get. My mom had big hopes for me."

"Big hopes in the sense that she wanted you to strive to achieve what she never did or did you have the feeling that she just thought it was wonderful that you would have more opportunities than her?"

"A combination of the two, I think. My mom was a very compassionate person who helped wherever she could, but I also think she had bigger dreams for herself than what life gave her."

"Did anything particular happen to stop her from achieving her goals?"

"Yes, she became pregnant when she was very young. She'd just turned 16. So even though she loved me and always supported me, I must have been her ball and chain, arriving as early as I did."

"So, she gave up on educating herself?"

"Yes, it was hard with a young child, and the war years were lean, so she helped wherever she could and poured her energy into the neighbourhood. She was rewarded with a shilling here and there."

"What was your relationship with your dad like?"

"It was good but also a little cold. My dad was an incredibly honourable man who took responsibility for his actions. A Christian man."

"You say that he took responsibility for his actions. Does that mean that he took responsibility for you after having been with your mom?"

"Definitely. My parents weren't planning to get married, but when my mom got pregnant, my dad took responsibility for his actions and married my mom so he could provide for her and for me. That meant a lot to my mom. If my dad hadn't taken on that responsibility, she would've been in a bad position. Back then, being alone with a child at such a young age would've been very hard."

"Indeed, those conditions would've been trying."

"My dad was a friendly and helpful man, but he might have chosen to do things differently if I hadn't been in the picture."

"So, there wasn't that much love between your parents but rather a practical arrangement?"

"I considered their relationship to be a good partnership. They were friendly towards each other, and all in all, I had a comfortable upbringing without too many fights, but there probably wasn't that much love between them." Klara pauses before continuing. "When I used the world 'cold' to describe my relationship with my dad, I think that was mainly because he was worried about me. He was worried that I would make irreversible mistakes. That was especially true when I hit puberty and started being interested in boys. He tried to limit my access to them. I was always the one with the earliest curfew when we had a dance, for example. It wasn't a punishment, so much as a hope that I would be careful because he knew just how things could go wrong."

"Was he a little reprimanding?"

"Yes. I've always been nervous about disappointing him because it was very important to him that I wouldn't make a mistake of the same calibre."

"How did that affect you in your teenage years?"

"I was a sensible girl, but I also had dreams of rebelling. I wanted to try out the adventure that my friends were telling me about."

"In terms of school and education, what were your dreams?"

"I really wanted to get into sixth form and get my diploma. Getting an education was very important to me."

"Did something happen that prevented you from achieving that goal?"

"Um, yes, you could say that."

"Is it something you want to tell me about?"

"Yes, I'd love to. It's nice to finally have someone to talk to."

The Fatal Summer

"Hmm, so, where to begin…" Klara pauses briefly before continuing. "Well, it was the summer before high school. Early one night, I go to the beach with my friends. There are a lot of people there, and most of them have brought blankets and are sitting around, talking in their groups. Some people have even built bonfires. We stand there and look around, and before long, I spot Karl."

"Who's Karl?"

"Karl was from Copenhagen, and he was one year older than me. He was on vacation with his family. He was going to be in town for three weeks, and he didn't know anyone there."

"How old were you at this time?"

"I was almost 16."

"Okay. Continue."

"He caught my eye because I thought he looked very exotic."

"Exotic?"

"Yes, he had dark hair and brown eyes. We didn't see that much back in the day. We got to talking, and he told me that he looked the way he did because his dad was from Greece.

His mom was from Copenhagen. They had met each other at the Greek Embassy."

"Was he good company?"

"Yes, he was good company," Klara says with a smile. "I spent a lot of time looking at him that evening, and when it looked like he was about to leave, I plucked up the courage to walk over to him; I was very nervous." Klara looks down at her hands. "He told me that he should be getting home soon, and I tell him that I'm not allowed to be out for very long, so I needed to get going too. He offered to walk me home, and even though I was nervous, I accepted the offer. We talked most of the way, and he was very polite and incredibly interesting. He had travelled a lot, and I had never travelled. We decided that I'd be showing him around town one of the coming days, and after that, we parted ways."

"Had you had a boyfriend by this point?"

"No, this was my first time."

"So, you ended up dating?"

"For the summer, yes. He came to my house after lunch the following day. My dad was at work, but my mom was home. She looks a little pensive, but she gives me permission to show him around." Klara pauses. "That marks the beginning of the best three weeks of my life."

"Did your dad know you were seeing each other during those three weeks?"

"Yes. I introduce him to Karl halfway through his vacation. He doesn't seem too excited, but Karl is so polite and proper; he gets permission to ask me out. On one of his last nights in town, he accompanies me to a dance."

"What happened after those three weeks?"

"I've fallen deeply in love with him, but I know that we don't have a future together. At least not immediately, because he's moving to Greece for two years after the summer vacation."

"He's moving to Greece?"

"Yes, because of his dad's work. He was moving away for at least two years, and he would be studying down there."

"So, you weren't expecting to see him again?"

"I hoped to, and we decided to write to each other and go on as pen pals and see what happened."

"So, Karl goes back to Copenhagen, and the summer vacation is almost over. Then what happens?"

"I discover that I'm pregnant." Klara looks back down at her hands in her lap.

"Oh, wow…"

"That was how I felt too," Klara says with a small smile. "We were together on his last day. Together in that way, I mean…I wanted to, but I just was not prepared for the consequences at the time. I panicked and thought that this will significantly limit the opportunities I have in the future. I knew my parents were set on me getting an education, and that's what I want too. I don't want to be a mom at 16."

"Just like your mom."

"Yes."

"What did you do next?"

"I chose to not tell my parents. I was scared of their reaction. I hoped that I'd made a mistake. That everything would go back to the way it was. I was too scared to write to Karl too. He was in Greece and had started his studies. I didn't want to limit him or his opportunities. I knew how badly he wanted to go out and experience the world. I was also scared that he'd ignore my situation and continue living his life in Greece without having any contact with me." Klara pauses. "I'd started school, and I had horrible nausea. One day when I was in the restroom, a girl from one of the other classes heard me throwing up. She asked me if I was pregnant, and I obviously told her that I'm not. Still, she tells me that her sister had been in a similar situation and that she went to get help in a house in another town. I almost ran out of the restroom without responding to her, but after a couple of weeks, I start to feel the first signs of life inside me, and I decided to wait for her outside the school. She saw me immediately and walked over. I didn't say anything to her. I just nodded, and she told me to come with her. We went back to her house, and her sister told me about this place…I tell her that I don't want to have the child and that I don't want to give it up for adoption. She tells me that they can help me in other ways…even though it's illegal."

"Then what did you do?"

"I got the address, and they told me how to get there. It was a secret place, so I wasn't allowed to tell anyone about it, and I couldn't use my real name while I was there. And then they told me that I needed to bring money."

"Where did you get money from?"

"I took the money my mom saved in the cookie jar in the kitchen."

"Did your mom know that you took the money?"

"I asked her if I could borrow money. When she asked me what I needed to borrow it for, I answered that it was for something important. My mom looked at me for a long time, and I honestly don't know if she'd figured out the situation

I'm in. She didn't say anything, just gave me the cookie jar and left the kitchen."

"Then what did you do?"

"I took the money and left the next day. I was banking on being back home later the same day. I went to the small house in the middle of a field. There were no houses nearby, so nobody saw me arrive."

Panic at The Dinner Table

"Did they make you feel welcome?"

"Yes, they did. They told me to have a seat while I waited. The doctor wouldn't be there until later. I handed my money over to a woman. I think she was the one who lived in the house. There were two other girls besides me. I think we were in the same situation. We didn't wait long when there was finally a knock on the door; it was a man carrying a brown leather bag. Then we were shown to a room further down the hallway." Klara pauses. "I was last, and it was a horrible experience sitting there, hearing the others cry. By the time it was my turn, I'm terrified."

"How many times did you consider leaving the house?"

"Many times. So many times…"

"But you stuck to your decision?"

"Yes, but I shouldn't have." Klara pauses again. "I was asked to go into a room and lie down on the table. I think it was a dinner table. I take off my underpants, and a man took out a knitting needle and a lamp…Then I remembered an awful sharp pain, and then I fainted…When I woke up again, I was bathed in blood. The doctor and the woman who lives in the house were cleaning up the blood, but they couldn't stop the bleeding. I almost panicked, and I could tell by the look on their faces that they were both very nervous. I got tired and cold, and then I died…"

"So, you died on the dinner table?"

"Yes." Klara sits there for a while without saying another word.

"When did you realise that you were dead?"

"Almost immediately, I think."

"What was that experience like for you?"

"The world was spinning, but all of a sudden, everything went still, and I was no longer in pain. When I looked around, I could suddenly see myself and the others from outside. Or from above, rather. As if I was floating around the room. It was very unusual." Klara offers a slight smile.

"How did the woman and the man react?"

"I could see that they were very nervous. They looked around as if to make sure that nobody had seen what was going on. When I was bleeding profusely, I remember them asking me if I told anyone that I was there, and I said no. Nobody knew."

"Then what did they do?"

"They bury my body in the field in the middle of the night. They were scared of getting caught because what they had done was strictly illegal. I watched myself being put into the ground. It made me feel all numb and very disoriented. When the sun rose again, I was sitting alone in the field. I was thinking that maybe this was all a bad dream. I walked around for a while wondering what to do next. Then I spotted a house not too far away. I stayed close to that house for a long time. I don't know how long exactly because the days didn't feel the same anymore."

"What's this house that you stayed close to?"

"It's this house that we're in right now. I was here the day Charlotte moved in with her two kids. She...she reminds me of my mom." Klara sniffles.

"In what way?"

"She has the same energy. The same compassionate nature. I could feel that Charlotte wouldn't have it in her to send me away so long as I didn't cause her any trouble..."

Klara sits for a while without talking.

"I miss my mom."

"Why didn't you try to go home to your parents?"

"I've been gathering up the courage, but I'm still not fully there." Klara falls quiet again. "If I'm being honest, it's probably because I'm ashamed."

"You end up in the same situation as your mom, and yet you're ashamed? Are you ashamed that you copied your mom?"

"My mom chose to have me – no matter the consequences. I wasn't brave enough to do that. My mom has always told me that she would've had me whether my dad had stood by her side or not. I didn't have that bravery and ability to make sacrifices. I wanted to see the world. There was so much I wanted to do. So, I'm ashamed that I wasn't as strong as my mom...That I was selfish and didn't want the ball and chain in the form of a child."

"What do you think has been the hardest part about all this?"

"That I've made a mistake that I can never fix."

In a quiet voice, Laurens says, "Your story shows how hard it can be when you don't have someone to turn to, or if you don't have someone that you feel like you can ask for help. The things you really struggle to talk to your parents about are often the most important. That was especially true in your day. You end up making a decision that has such severe consequences for you that you actually end up losing your life."

"Yes, that wasn't the plan."

"No, I don't think it was."

"I just wanted to go out and try all these things that my parents had told me about. I wanted to go out and conquer the world, and then I end up here."

"The way I see it, you have nothing to be ashamed of. I think your mom feels the same way because, in a way, you've followed in her footsteps, so I think she would understand."

"Maybe, but we'll probably never know."

"I don't know about that. I feel like someone is here to talk to you."

Reunited Without Anger

Laurens steps aside, and Klara's mom steps into the living room. Klara doesn't look at her mom, instead keeping her eyes fixed guiltily on her hands.

"My dear child," Klara's mom says as she walks over to Klara with her arms stretched out in front of her. "I've been so nervous and so scared thinking about what happened to you." She wraps Klara in her arms, and the tears stream down her face. "You never came back that day, and I've always wondered what happened seeing as you just left. What could've possibly been so bad that you couldn't share it with me?"

"You're not mad at me?"

"Of course not. I'm worried and sad. We looked for you for the longest time, but as the years went by, we gave up hope of ever finding you. I wish you'd confided in me or in us. It wouldn't have been ideal, but both your dad and I would've been there for you, and we would've found a solution."

Laurens looks at Klara.

"How do you feel now, looking back on your life and your choices?"

"Making the right decision can be incredibly hard. Sometimes it might feel like you were made to take care of other people. But I don't think you can be good at caring for someone else if you're miserable on the inside. It's hard to balance fulfilling your duties with choosing yourself and staying focused on what's best for yourself. I didn't know the consequences of my choice, and things had worked out for the big sister of the girl I talked to at school. So back then, I guess I thought that all I had to do was survive a few days of pain, and then I'd be free to live my life. I'd be on my way towards a career and all these opportunities…Looking back, it feels so stupid."

"Yeah, but life is unpredictable, and you don't always know the consequences. You're a good example of that. We can only make our decisions based on the situations we find ourselves in. I'm sure that you made the decision that felt right to you at the time. And maybe that's the best we can do."

"Yes, I think it's all about getting the most out of whatever situation you find yourself in, even if it's not the situation you wanted. You can still have a happy life. But that's hard to think about when you're 16."

"You don't know that much about life at 15 or 16. You sort of have to feel your way through life. And sometimes you make a mistake, especially when you don't have anyone – or think you don't have anyone – you can ask for help."

Klara looks at her mom.

"Yes."

"Come, my child, it's time for us to leave. They're waiting for us."

"Waiting? Who's waiting?"

"You'll see. You'll be so happy," Klara's mom answers.

Klara leaves the room with her mom, and as they leave, they become blurrier.

Laurens looks over at Charlotte.

"How do you feel?"

"I see the parallels between Klara's life and my own. I was used to taking care of my siblings from a young age, but I had a hard time accepting my mom's expectations and ambitions for my life and what I would become. She often told me that I shouldn't make the same mistake as her. I felt like it was hard to live up to her expectations, and I found it hard to talk to her about it. I didn't want to disappoint her and cause her any trouble. She had enough on her mind as it was. I need to think about the expectations I have for my kids. They're going to make mistakes like everyone else, so maybe I should just hope that they trust me. That they feel like they can come to me with their problems. That way I might be able to help them or give them advice."

"Yeah, I think that's a great place to start. Their lives are what they are, and they have to learn from that and their mistakes but hopefully without suffering consequences as serious as Klara's."

Chapter 3
Rashid's Dilemma
Dare to Choose with Your Heart

An Afghan family in Copenhagen have reached out for help because someone is watching them in their apartment. The ghost that appears comes bearing a tragic story and a burning desire to get his message across. How far should you be willing to go when it comes to reason and emotions?

When Pernille and Laurens arrived at the apartment where a divorced mother lives with her three daughters and two sons, it isn't long before they sense the energy of a sceptical and withdrawn man.

"Who are you?" Laurens asks.

Nobody says anything in the apartment.

"Why are you here?"

"I'm not sure I want to tell you that," a voice says.

"Why not?"

"I'm not sure you'll understand."

"What's your name?"

"Rashid."

"Okay, Rashid, but what is it that you think we won't understand?"

"You're from another culture that's different from ours in many ways."

"You might be right about that, but I still think we should give it a shot. It's all about getting your message across to the family. That's why we're here, right?"

"Correct."

"Good. Now, where are you from?"

"Afghanistan?"

"What was your childhood like?"

"I grew up in a period of turbulence when the Russians occupied Afghanistan, only to eventually be replaced by religious groups, tribes, and warlords. That greatly affects the area I'm from. We're a family of 13. My mom and dad and my 10 siblings and me."

"Is it normal to have such a big family at the time?"

"Yes, having many children is normal, especially in the countryside."

"What's the gender distribution like?"

"We have six boys and five girls. So, we're a blessed family with lots of boys."

"What about the age distribution?"

"There are about 20 years between the eldest and the youngest, and I'm right in the middle. I'm the first child of my dad's second wife. My dad's first wife died of complications after having given birth. My dad marries someone younger, and they have six kids together."

"So, you're the first child with his new wife. Were men allowed to have multiple wives at the time?"

"Yes, that's relatively normal."

"But your dad only has one at a time?"

"Yes."

"What did your father do?"

"He made shoes and other leather goods, like protective aprons for blacksmiths and other craftsmen. He was good with his hands."

"Was he self-employed or employed?"

"He was self-employed."

"What did your mom do?"

"It's normal for women to stay at home, so that's what both my dad's first wife and my mom did."

"I guess there's enough to do with a family of that size."

"Yes, there was always something that needs doing."

"What was your family status like? What kind of means did you have? Were things fine or did you struggle economically?"

"We were pretty comfortable. That was part of the reason my mom is such a good match. You have to have something to offer if a family of higher social status is going to give their daughter away to someone who already has five kids – that calls for a certain status. My dad provided for us, and we all got to go to school."

"How many years did you go to school?"

"Twelve. My parents, particularly my mom who came from a wealthier family, were adamant about us getting an education and excelling. I'd say we were a little more modern and had more opportunities than other people in our village. When I was around 18 years old, I travelled to the big city to attend the university."

"Did you live alone?"

"No, at first I moved in with my older brother who's about ten years older than me, as well as his wife and kids."

"How did living together work out for you?"

"It was fine; we have a good relationship with each other. He's educated as well, and we had many interesting conversations about life, the stars, history, culture, and the possibilities of the future."

"So, things were good in spite of the unrest in your country?"

"I think we made the most of what we had."

"How old are you when you finish your degree?"

"I was in my mid-20s."

"What was the atmosphere like in the city?"

"There was a lot of unrest. Aside from the Russians, the religious groups, like the Taliban, were fighting for power, and the religious undertones were starting to affect the atmosphere in the city."

"How did you feel about that?"

"I think religion is a good thing if it lifts a population but a bad thing if it represses. The religious sentiment that rose in our time was repressive, and it led to a series of conflicts in our social circle. I married a woman as educated as myself. I noticed that the people who were considered modern before the political unrest started to force their daughters and wives to cover up and encouraged me to do the same."

"What did you do? Did you force your wife to cover up?"

"Absolutely not."

"What happened for you and your wife? Did you still live with your brother?"

"I stayed with my brother while I was getting an education. It was not customary to live by yourself. You stayed with your family until you got married and started a family of your own. In some cases, couples even chose to stay with one side of the family after they've gotten married. It's not like in Europe where you move away from home and one man lives here and one woman lives there."

"So, you stayed in the city?"

"No. My wife and I left the country. She was a doctor and was offered a position in London."

"Was it just you and your wife or did you have kids?"

"It's just me and my wife. We have no kids."

"What was your experience in London?"

"It was very exciting and educational but also incredibly different, seeing as we were so used to being surrounded by family. It doesn't take us long to get involved with some of the Afghan communities, but we still struggled a lot. There were those who wanted to assimilate, and then there were those who clung to the old traditions. We wanted a bit of both worlds – the best of both cultures."

"Did you manage?"

"Sort of."

"How were things on the family front? Did you have kids by now?"

"Yes, we had two girls, and we lived a modern English life and raised our girls so they knew their Afghan roots, but we never demanded a certain type of attitude or behaviour from them. The way we saw it, we had a solid hold on both cultures. Slowly, however, we came to realise that not everyone felt the same way about our lifestyle. In many people's eyes, we were too English."

"So, your daughters got to pick their own culture?"

"Yes, we have always valued personal freedom, and we believe we had made the best decision for our daughters. But it's a decision I ended up regretting."

"Why?"

"Because as our children grew up, more and more Afghan immigrants came to England. A lot of the young people had an old-fashioned view of women and their rights. Our modern philosophy made us stick out like a sore thumb. Our daughters wanted to keep the old culture as their primary culture, so they sought out suitable husbands in the Afghan community. But they were met with criticism and judgment for being too modern, and rumour had it that they were no longer modest because they had been given such loose reins. And that means that none of the Afghan families wanted their sons to marry them."

No Man's Land for the Daughters

"So, in spite of the fact that you were thousands of miles away from your home country, its culture still affected your lives."

"Yes, things changed a lot while we were there. We came to England because of the job opportunities, but as time goes by, groups of refugees started to arrive. People who have been shaped by a culture dictated by the Taliban and a strict regime, where controlling your daughters was a prerequisite for them getting married. It had literally been beaten into them because where they came from, you got lashings in the street if you weren't covered up enough. Seeing modern Afghan girls getting an education and wanting an Afghan husband was a culture shock. Many of them struggled to accept the freedom that my daughters expected their husbands to give them. The contrast between my daughters' lifestyle and the attitudes of their potential husbands was too sharp."

"How did you and your wife feel at the time? Did you think they'd figure it out because that's what we do in Europe, or did you want them to find a husband sooner rather than later?"

"We wanted both of our children to meet a man who respected their freedom but still had a link to the old culture, so the family legacy carried on. A modern life where they knew their roots. We wanted them to choose their own husbands, but we also didn't want them to become part of a family that didn't know anything about the Afghan culture. We were worried that they would both meet a man who's been too shaped by the religious undercurrent created by the Taliban. A man who wanted to control his wife and children, so they didn't lose their modesty, as they called it. We were very scared that they would meet someone who smiled and said, 'Of course, you should keep working, and of course, you should stick with your education,' and then slam all those doors shut as soon as they were married. We have seen it happen to others. There was often a lively debate in my daughters' social circle about what you can and can't do, which is something the average Englishman didn't care about. He'd probably consider our daughters to be on the boring or well-behaved end of the spectrum. They behaved and dressed nicely – never with a plunging neckline and never showing their thighs – but still, they were loose in our fellow countrymen's eyes."

"In other words, they ended up in a kind of no man's land when it came to potential husbands?"

"Of course, there were those who supported their lifestyle, but they were few and far between, and my daughters faced a lot of defeat. With great sorrow, we watched as our two strong, talented, and extroverted girls became more and more introverted, and their confidence started to falter."

"How old were your daughters when the conflicts started to arise?"

"16 and 17. They hadn't started looking for husbands, but other families had begun to look around for suitable matches for their children. That's when they really started to gossip."

"So, that's when the culture started to show its teeth?"

"I guess you could say that, yes. When my daughters were around 20 years old, they started to want husbands. They didn't necessarily want to get married immediately, but they did want to get engaged with a view of getting married, but the community gossiped about them."

"What did you do about the gossip? Did you manage to stay out of it?"

"I tried out various strategies. At first, I withdrew from the community, but that made them gossip even more. Then I tried to get more involved, so they could get to know me, and I can speak on behalf of my daughters. I was met with a lot of understanding. 'You're a good man, Rashid,' they said. 'You've taken good care of your daughters, so I'm sure they're good too, but we'll have to turn you down. We don't want to risk our family being subject to all this gossip.'"

"Did you talk to your daughters about the issue?" Laurens asks.

"My wife talked to them a lot, and the situation broke her heart. I sometimes spoke to them too, but they got shy because they knew how much I hear from the community."

"It's interesting because your daughters were a good match in terms of status and employment. I imagine your finances were good, and that you had a comfortable life in London?"

"Yes, my wife worked at a renowned hospital, and I taught mathematics at the university."

"So, they were a good match when it came to finances and status but not so much in terms of culture?"

"Finances were important to everyone, including my countrymen, but a woman's modesty was more important to them. You could be as rich as you wanted, but if you had brought shame on your family and lost your innocence, your honour, then you were worthless."

"So, I imagine that the men and families who had considered your daughters had found themselves in a bit of dilemma?"

"I think so because we did get the occasional negotiation going. You met the family and visited them for tea so you could talk, and the families braced themselves for the way things are heading. The girls adjusted to the idea of their husband's name and where they'd be living. But then, out of nowhere, it all stopped: 'We don't want this after all', and then all communication ceases, and you never spoke to that family again. It happened more than once that my daughters were given hope, only to be rejected, and they took that very personally. They knew that the rejection was the result of them being too liberal and that the families didn't want to commit to the risk of fraternising with them."

The Double Rejection

"Did you feel pressured by the situation?"

"There was a lot of pressure, but all of a sudden, we thought it's happening for both of them. They were 23 and 24 at this point. But within two days of each other, both suitors rejected them. We were very sad on their behalf, and my wife and I had a big conversation about how it's a good thing that the girls are so strong and that they will make it through. But they don't take the rejection lightly, and that's when the nightmare happened. They took their own lives."

"Oh, wow. Did they do it together or separately?"

"Together... They took pills."

"Did they do it at home or somewhere in town?"

"They rented a hotel room and left us a letter. They told us that they had made the decision together and that they wanted to leave this world together. They wrote that they had rented a room because they didn't want us to find them."

"What happened inside you?"

"I broke. Plain and simple!"

"I completely understand that. What were you thinking? How did you and your wife react? I can imagine that the grief swallowed you whole."

"I don't remember the time that followed. It's all a blur to me, and eight months later, my wife was diagnosed with breast cancer. I think it was brought on by the shock of losing the girls. We sort of fled into her treatment and turned that into our project. She died 13 months later."

"Those were hard years. First, you lost your daughters and then your wife."

"It was a very difficult time."

"What did your family in Afghanistan have to say about it all?"

"My family was spread out across Europe because of the state of our home country. A lot of well-established families had chosen to leave. I had a younger sister in Denmark, a brother and sister in Sweden and a bunch of family in Germany."

"How did your family respond to your situation, to your grief?"

"With great horror."

"So, there was a lot of understanding and compassion? Did anyone say, 'If only you had limited them a little' and 'Maybe you were a little too liberal' and 'We probably would have done things this way'?"

"Yes. There were many well-meaning reprimands, but they didn't change anything. My head was filled with 'What if's…I would have done anything to change the situation."

"What were the reactions like in your community? How did your surroundings, your culture, and the families who knew your daughters respond?"

"The reactions were mixed. Everything from horror to understanding. Horror that they would take such a drastic step and understanding that you're better off being released from the pain of not being able to have your own family than to live a life without a husband and children."

"Those were difficult odds to be faced with. What did you do with the chaos that I assume you were feeling? I imagine you could barely breathe?"

"I started feeling a pinch in my chest, like something was weighing me down. The doctor told me that it was grief and stress and that I needed to get away to find some peace and quiet."

"How old were you at this point?"

"Around 46–48 years old. I was on sick leave from the university and had been for a while, partly due to my wife's illness. So, I decided to take a sabbatical indefinitely, and my younger sister who lived near Copenhagen invited me to come stay with her, so that's what I ended up doing."

"What was the status of your sister's life?"

"She was divorced and lived alone with her two children, a boy and a girl. She was a schoolteacher at a private school where she taught languages."

"Did the act of you moving in affect her situation in any way?"

"No, there weren't any problems seeing as I'm an older brother. In our culture, it's very normal for an older brother, uncle or man from the family to step in and take over responsibility of the family in case of death, divorce, and so on. Not that I actually had to, because it was pretty normal to be divorced in Denmark in the 90s. My younger sister had refugee status because she had stayed in our home country for much longer and had married an Afghan man before they moved to Denmark together."

"So, she brought her husband with her?"

"Yes, they arrived together and were both granted refugee status, but they were later divorced."

"So, it helps the overall reputation when you step in and take over responsibility as a man of the family?"

"Yes."

"What's it like for you in Denmark?"

"It's a relief because I don't have to see anyone I already know. I was surrounded by looks of compassion in my community in London. A lot of people in the area, not to mention my entire network, knew what had happened, so my grief was constantly being triggered by their looks and questions. In Copenhagen, I was a nobody, and I had my sister to help. It gave my life meaning and substance again."

"How long did you stay with your sister?"

"Not that long...As the weeks and months went by, my chest pains worsened, especially during sudden exertion like running for a bus. It felt like I was being stabbed in the heart. I think the grief had weakened my heart. It's almost like it didn't want to beat anymore."

"That's understandable. Living through more than two years of emotional chaos where you barely dare to breathe has to take its toll."

Heart or Mind

"What's your time in Denmark like? Did you establish a new network?"

"As I didn't have a job in Denmark, most of the people I met were from my sister's social circle, and most of them are from Afghanistan. It reminded me of England. A lot of them have a modern approach to life and were mostly liberated, but the cultural heritage stopped them from going all the way – they kept each other in check through gossip, and I found that disgraceful."

"So, things were quite good, but there were still some cultural highlights or rituals, for example when it came to getting married, where they continued to choose the heritage over going down the new route?" Laurens asks.

"Yes and no. There were people who broke from the cultural norm, but they were also the ones who became the subject of criticism, so you had to know where you stood because as soon as you developed a bad reputation, it was almost impossible to fix it again. So, a lot of people limited themselves and their children to safeguard themselves against the gossip," Rashid explains.

"That sounds difficult to navigate, and my philosophy is that someone always bears the brunt of the criticism when nobody knows which road to take. How do you feel about the culture given the consequences it has had for you?"

"There's a conflict between my heart and my mind. My heart continues to demand freedom at all costs, but my mind wants me to just conform. The war between my heart and sense of reason continued to rage through the years – should you listen to reason and allow yourself to be limited so you can have a mediocre future, or should you follow your heart and aim for the stars, risking everything as you go along? As long as I lived, I never found the answer."

"How long were you in Denmark before you died?"

"I don't make it back to England. I had only been in Denmark for six months when I died."

"How did you die?"

"I collapsed in the stairwell of my sister's building, in the middle of carrying two grocery bags up to the fourth floor. An ambulance is called, but I died of heart failure on the way to the hospital before my 50th birthday."

"How did you get in touch with the family you're currently staying with?"

"One day, I met the mother on the train, on her way to negotiate on behalf of her daughters. It captivated my interest, and I wanted to follow her to see what happened. I watched as the same thing that happened to my daughters was happening to hers, so I tried to follow her home to wake her up. I wanted to tell her that she needs to pay attention to the struggle between her heart and her mind."

"It's interesting to think about, this conflict between the heart and the mind. There are a lot of feelings at stake."

"Yes, it's a bit of a balancing act, and the solution is often difficult – more difficult than you can imagine…How long can you be strong and alone? After our conversation today, I think the girls will think, 'Yes, we can do it', but the question is how long that feeling remains. I don't have the solution; I just want to make them aware of the problem."

"The way I see it, you've left your mark and made a valiant attempt to do something about the problem, only it had huge consequences. And it looks like you're stuck between this life and the next because of your grief."

"It's a mixture of grief and feeling guilty. On one hand, I should have done better by my kids, and on the other, the heart is the most important thing. It's still an active conflict for me."

"Do you know how that conflict started?"

"I was searching and mediating, but my fellow countrymen informed me that you can't come up to God unless you follow the rules that they've set. So, my conclusion was that since I couldn't leave this place and God wouldn't take me, I had probably failed."

"So, at the end of the day, it's about the fight between the established order and the liberated heart?"

"Yes, and the daughters in this house have hopes and dreams, but they're willing to push them aside in order to get married. They're also willing to make themselves smaller just to fit into another family, and that goes against what I believe. I understand them on a logical level, but how much should you be willing to conform? The daughters find themselves in exactly the same situation as mine...they want the new life but are caught in between that and the old ways, and they've experienced being rejected in the final second because it turned out that they weren't a good match. That's hard to cope with, and in the long run, it means that you let go of the values, dreams, and ambitions that guided the whole thing to begin with."

Dies of Grief

Rashid pauses briefly and continues.

"It's hard to see the success when my wife died of grief in the aftermath of our only two children ending their lives."

"You died of the same exact grief."

"Yes, my heart didn't want to go on without the three of them...without them, there was nothing more to life."

"It's a fate you wouldn't wish on your worst enemy, but it happens to you."

"Right. In the beginning, I felt like I had to go out and take God's punishment, that I wasn't orthodox enough to be accepted into His kingdom. That's why I started to push the mother and her daughters to become more orthodox and start to conform, otherwise nobody would want them. But after our conversation, I see that you have to follow your heart...but that's hard to do, and I haven't found the truth."

"Is there anything you regret in this life?"

"I regret many things. I regret not raising my daughters correctly in the eyes of the orthodox community. That could have secured both of their futures. I've regretted that for a long time."

"But you followed your heart, and sometimes that has unimaginable consequences."

"Unfortunately, yes."

"I can feel that someone has come to tell you something."

Laurens steps aside to let them through. Rashid's wife and two daughters have come to pick him up. They run towards him and lock him in their embrace.

"It's good to see you again. I've been longing to be reunited. What a bumpy road," Rashid's wife said.

"Yes, but I thought it was God's punishment to keep me here. That I wasn't worthy."

"Don't think such things. You're more than worthy."

"Yes, and you're an incredibly worthy father. You tried to show us how to follow our hearts, but we didn't understand, and that's not your fault because you did what you could in spite of the circumstances you were raised in," the two daughters say.

"I see now that it wasn't God's punishment keeping me here, but rather my own guilt, shame, and grief weighing me down so much, I couldn't leave."

"We've come to pick you up if you want to come with us," Rashid's wife and two daughters say.

Rashid looks at them and smiles, then he looks at Pernille and Laurens.

"Is there anything you want to say before you leave with your family?" Laurens asks.

"Yes." Rashid turns to the family living in the apartment. "God won't punish you for not following the orthodox rules, but your own feelings of being inadequate in life will. So, if you feel the presence of the deceased around you, it isn't necessarily because you've done something wrong but because there's an unresolved matter hanging over the deceased and weighing them down. You can help them let go of that. Nobody is cast out from the afterlife. Learning means making mistakes, but it's also the path towards development."

"Thank you for coming by and bringing the family's attention to the conflict between the heart and the mind. Enjoy the afterlife," Laurens says.

Rashid and his family leave the room, and they fade out as they walk.

Laurens looks at the family and asks, "How do you feel?"

"Weird but good."

"Do you see the similarities between your life and Rashid's?"

They nod, and we talk about their conflict and how they can create a new path that allows them to follow their hearts and reach for their dreams.

Chapter 4
The Baker's Passion
Never Let Anger Ruin Your Dreams

Since opening his store, Søren has been banking on healthier products and personal service. His dream is to create a store where people come before products, but something is standing in his way. He feels a sense of heaviness on the premises, his employees complain about headaches, and it's hard to get people to come into the store even though it's on the most visited part of the shopping street. The fact that there's a national chain with a similar range of products a little further down the street doesn't help either. Søren decides to do something about it. Before long, a ghost appears and reminds us that we can't change anything when we're angry.

After a short tour around the beautiful and inviting store, Pernille and Laurens begin to feel the sense of heaviness that Søren and his employees have talked about.

"Who are you, and what do you want?" Laurens says to the room, when he senses a presence.

"None of your business," an angry and frustrated voice responds.

"Can I ask what your name is?" Laurens tries carefully.

"You can call me the baker," the ghost says with some hesitation.

"All right. But I think you're here for a reason."

"Yes, can't you see that people are walking around like zombies? They walk the same paths they always walk, and they only see the path and nothing else as if they have tunnel vision," the baker says angrily.

"What do you mean?"

"Just look at Søren who owns this place. He's got a nice, new shop, but he's new in town. His vision is great, but people don't want to see it. They just want to keep doing what they've always done. They follow the path to the old store without thinking about what they buy and where they buy it from. They listen to their heads – to the habit – and do what they always do without stopping to think for a second and ask their heart what it really wants. If they did that, their heart would be startled and confused because it's not used to being asked for its opinion, and all of a sudden, it would have to come up with a wish. We walk around thinking we're oh-so-liberated, but we're creatures of habit. We're educated, talented, and modern when it comes to our culture, but my message is that we aren't as free as we think because our entire lives revolve around the input and habits we develop through media, ads, traditions, and all these things that tell us what quality products to buy. We're slaves to these sources of influence, and we don't stop to give new things a chance."

"You're right about that. People are so stressed and under so much pressure, they don't have the energy to stop and think about what they want to do with their lives," Laurens says and continues. "Where did you grow up?"

"In a small town not too far from here," the baker answers.

"What's your family like? Your mom and dad? Do you have siblings?"

"I grew up with both my parents, and I have an older brother who's about two years older than me."

"What was life like for your family?"

"I was born at the turn of the century, and I grew up in a good, relaxed family where my upbringing was unproblematic. My dad was a blacksmith and had his own forge, and my mom was a part-time music and vocal teacher. She helped out at the local church where she played the piano and organ, and she sang in the choir. The atmosphere at home was good, and we had a good relationship. We were privileged at a time where a lot of mothers stayed at home. My mom worked part-time, so she brought in some money. She was known for being a modern woman because she had an artistic side and was in the local church choir, so we were part of the community."

"What was school like for you?"

"My grades were average, and I was a good student, but the school didn't have my full attention. I was good with my hands, so I just wanted to get school out of the way. It didn't really interest me."

"You wanted to get it out of the way so you could go out and do what you wanted?"

"Yeah…I had a tightknit group of friends, five boys who hung out a lot, and after school, we went out to play. When we got older, we all started to spend more time helping out at home, so we could learn the family business. In my case, that was smithing. As soon as he was tall enough to reach over the counter, my good friend Hans started helping out his dad who was a grocer, and before long, he was a delivery boy. One of my other friends was good with horses, his dad was a stableman who worked for a rich gentleman on the outskirts of town who had some gorgeous horses. My friend joined his dad in the stables early on, when he was about eight or ten years old. Our parents told us that when we help out, we don't misbehave, and there's plenty to do because we didn't have any of these modern resources at the time."

Born into the Business

"How did you imagine the future when you were a boy?"

"We talked about the future a lot, but it didn't take me long to realise that the path had been laid for us. Jens, the stableman's son, had already been told that he'd start as an assistant when his dad was starting to get old, and that he'd take over when his dad retired. He liked horses, so it just felt like a bonus to him. He was born into the business, and his dad had paved the way for him, so his future was set, and he was excited for it. But I had this game that I liked to play where you think about what you would do if you could choose to do anything, or which path you would take if your dad had a different job. A lot of my friends told me that they would choose the same path, but I always wondered whether that's actually the case or whether it's been so drilled into them that they can only see the path that's already in front of them. When I asked myself, I always answered that I'd want to be a baker...I've always loved food, or rather, I've always loved baked goods. I've always thought that bread is amazing and that you can do anything with bread. It combines all the best things. You can smell it, taste it, work with it, create it, and sell it. But I was met with resistance and wonder, and people telling me that Jakob's dad is the baker, so Jakob will be taking over the bakery business, and you can't just change your mind and do someone else's job."

"Were there other people who thought differently or were you alone?"

"I think I was the only one who questioned the way things were."

"Did you hang out with the baker's son?"

"No, I didn't, but I knew him. He was in my older brother's grade. The baker had multiple sons, by the way."

"How many years did you go to school?"

"Six years."

"What did you do once school was over?"

"I became my dad's apprentice."

"How old were you at the time?"

"I was 12 years old. My older brother was a working man, and he lived at the horse farm where he worked. He started learning the craft from my father when he was young, just like me, but they needed someone to tend to the house, fences, and machinery on the farm, so he took care of all that."

"Was there some sort of understanding that you would take over the forge now that your brother had chosen to do something different?"

"My parents saw it as a good source of income, and the families knew each other. My dad thought it would be good for my brother to go out and put his skills to the test and earn a living, and my dad still had me to take over the business when the time comes."

"How did you enjoy the apprenticeship?"

"It was fine, and I was pretty good at it, but I wouldn't have called it my passion. It was great to have a craft, but it didn't awaken all of my senses like baking does."

"Where did your interest in baking come from?"

"My mom is good at baking, and she loves it, but where I come from, only women bake at home. The men are the ones who open businesses and sell bread. I have always been very interested when my mom started baking breads and pretzels. I watched her and offered to help, and she thought it was nice that I was interested in that."

The Sign

"When did you first feel like maybe you should do something different?"

"The first time I really felt it was when my dad changed the sign outside to 'Jespersen & Son'. It made my stomach flip in the bad kind of way. On the one hand, I was proud because I knew that him putting my name on the sign meant that we were equals in the workplace, but it also sealed my fate."

"How old were you at this point?"

"I was in my late 20s, almost 30 years old."

"So, you spent a lot of years working with your father, and now you were being recognised as an equal. What was that like for you?"

"My dad didn't actually change the sign until a customer asked him why my name wasn't on the storefront after all these years. By this point, he'd already spent a lot of time talking about how I would one day take over the business, but

I'd always seen the blacksmith's life as being temporary. But now I really felt like it was time to try something different."

"Did it get harder to talk about it now that the sign was up?"

"A lot harder, because the entire town would be able to see that there was a conflict brewing if the sign needed to be changed. It was a small place, and we knew most of the people there because my mom went to the church and was a familiar face around town."

"How did you handle the situation?"

"I don't know. I didn't think I handled it at all; I just left it bottled up. I felt bad about it all because my dad was getting older and starting to talk about retiring and having me take over the family business. When I thought about the options and the idea of spending the rest of my life as a blacksmith, it was almost like I shut down completely."

"Your mom knew that you loved baking. Did your dad know too?"

"Yes, he knew. My mom often told him that I'd helped her with the bread, but I don't think it occurred to him that I might be thinking of doing something else with my life. It was not the norm, and unemployment rates were high in the 30s, so you were meant to just be happy that you had a job. I don't think it had ever crossed his mind that I might be wanting to do something else because a lot of people struggled to pay their bills, and, in his eyes, I was lucky enough to have a craft and a business that he'd already laid the foundation for. My dad had taught me his craft out of love and pride, and he had never tried to hide the fact that I was his son. And my older brother worked on the farm and had a good job there, so my dad saw us both as successful, and he was proud of what he had managed to teach us. Two hard-working boys with a good pair of hands…"

"What about the time after 'son' shows up on the sign? What was that like?"

"I grew more and more unhappy. Some might have called me angry and difficult."

"How did your mom, dad, and surroundings respond to that change? Perhaps you had a girlfriend at that point?"

"I had a wife, and we had been married for a couple of years by the time the sign went up. We had moved to a small house not too far from my parents', and she thought I had become angry and difficult."

"Could you talk to your wife about your desire to change careers?"

"I mentioned the fact that I wanted to do something completely different to her. She got stressed and worried that I'd throw away everything that we had and that it wouldn't work out if I did something different. She was worried about how we'd put food on the table. And I understood that, but I thought to myself that of course it would work out. As long as your heart is in it, anything will work out. At least, that's how I felt at the time."

"Did anyone come out in support of you?"

"I was still good friends with Hans who supported me and told me that I could do it, and that I should take the leap and try. Once in a while, he laughed at me but not in a mocking way. Mainly because he didn't think there's any reason to throw away what I have seeing as things were fine the way they were. He chuckled and told me that I'm going to make things hard for myself, but he still said that he supported me. Still, I don't think he understood how much I wanted it."

"You had been married for a couple of years, and things were going south. What did you do?"

"My dad got sick. He struggled with his back, and he was bedridden most of the time and ended up not being able to work all that much, so there I was, alone and trying to figure out how to handle the situation. I know that he had saved up for his old age, and I had been saving up to refurbish or open a store or do something else…I'd been dreaming of it for so long, but when my dad got sick, it really hit home that I'd be left alone with the business, and that made it even harder and also proved to me once and for all that it was not what I wanted. We had been working together all these years, and that has been pleasant because we had a good relationship." The baker pauses briefly. "Then one day, my dad announced that he can't work anymore and that he had to stay at home. Doctor Jensen had told him that he needed to stop working, otherwise he'll become disabled in his old age. His lower back had been worn down, and he can't do it anymore. He stooped and walked with a stick. My dad told me that it fell to me to take over the family business, and that shifted something inside me."

"So, this is it…The life that's been in the cards for you since you were 12 years old, the responsibility, the expectations, and the tradition. The life you've been trained for."

"I really wanted to tell him that I wanted to close the forge and refurbish it, but I never got around to it."

The Time Has Come

"How many years do you spend alone in the forge?"

"Two years, almost three…At that point, I was experiencing marital problems, and I have to admit that I was taking my own unhappiness out on my wife because I couldn't talk about the family legacy with the people that I actually needed to talk to. So, she was unhappy and threatened moving back in with her parents if I didn't pull myself together. But two or three years after my dad quit the forge, he died of a lung infection after a particularly rough winter. My mom was alone in the house, and I thought that it might be easier to have the conversation now that I no longer needed to confront my dad. The time had come for me to change careers if I wanted to…And I did."

"Did you do it immediately following his death, or did some time pass?"

"About half a year later, I removed the sign that says 'Jespersen & Son', and then I closed the forge and start to refurbish."

"What did your mom say?"

"I tell her shortly before the refurbishing began. The fact that I was erasing my dad's legacy came as a shock, and it made her deeply unhappy. She told me that she had always been proud to walk down the main street and look over at the forge that her husband had inherited from his father and that her own son was now running. I tried to tell her that it was not an idea that's come out of nowhere but one that had been on my mind for several years. I don't think she understood why I was closing a good, stable business and erasing a legacy seeing as I was good at the craft. She was scared that I would bring shame on my dad's legacy if I went out and did something else poorly. But I stuck to my guns, closed the forge, and refurbished it to something completely different, and it made me unbelievably happy and excited all at once. In fact, I was practically ecstatic. My wife thought I had gone crazy. She thought I was losing my mind. But the big day finally arrived when I put up the new sign and opened my business. My wife helped me out by serving the customers, and I baked the bread."

"So, you hadn't been trained as a baker, but you were passionate and you had some experience from helping out at home?"

"Yes, I had tried a few different things, found some good recipes, and used the recipes we had in the family. As I've mentioned, my mom was good at baking, so she helped me out with some advice as well, because even though she was sad and confused, she wanted me to succeed. So, I felt confident in my craft, and I chose to dive straight in, and one day, I opened the doors to my new store. There were lots of customers the first day, including some of my old friends. Most of them showed up because they wanted to see the new business, but they also bought bread and created a positive atmosphere. I was really excited, but after just two weeks, the novelty started to wear off, and after a month and a bit, the number of customers had dwindled significantly."

"Was there room for two bakers in town?"

"I thought so, seeing as the stores were on different sides of the town. I was really proud of my craft, and I saw each bread as a small piece of art. The experience of growing, smelling, and tasting them was amazing to me. I enjoyed baking them, and it felt like freedom in a way that I can't even describe. But as time went on, the number of customers continued to fall."

"What about your friends and your social circle?"

"A lot of people were surprised, and they didn't understand what I was doing. They all warned me that it was tough competition, seeing as there were third-generation bakers down the street. They asked me how I was going to compete with them, and I replied that I guess it's all about how the bread tastes. They shook their heads, but they continued to dutifully buy their bread from me."

"What were people saying about your bread?"

"I heard that they thought it's good bread. In fact, I didn't hear anyone say that it's bad."

"So, you were onto something in terms of quality?"

"That's what I thought, but over the course of the next six months, my turnover fell so much that I was struggling to make ends meet, and that stressed me out. All those years, I had walked around, convinced that this was my future."

"Did you ever consider going back to your old craft, maybe just on a part-time basis, to make ends meet? Surely, the situation was hard on your savings?"

"A lot of my old friends actually ask me why I didn't just go back to my old craft now that I had tried my hand at this. It probably wasn't all that sensible, but I couldn't imagine going back."

"How did your mom feel about it all?"

"The whole thing made her very sad."

"Did you feel guilty?"

"I guess I did. About the fact that reaching for my dreams had created so much confusion and frustration for the people closest to me. Mostly because they didn't understand what I was doing. My wife wasn't the only one who thought I was losing my mind anymore. Sometimes I thought it too. It was frustrating to break the mould like that, and I kept beating myself up with the fact that you don't close a third-generation store to try something new unless the old store has folded."

Anger Builds

"Did your wife soften up, or did she get more tense as the number of customers continued to fall?"

"She didn't understand my decision, and she found it difficult to accept that we had practically no resources. And I grew angrier by the day. One day, I saw the wife of one of my close friends walk past the store, and later that day, she returned with a bag from the other baker! I saw red because if those closest to me couldn't support me, then who would? In hindsight, I understand that it's nice to shop somewhere where people are happy and open when you have to go out and buy things in the morning. I was angry and full of pent-up frustration, and I noticed that it didn't matter if I had my door open so passers-by could smell my breads, or if I was in the store or put out signs. People continued to buy their bread from the third-generation baker instead of the blacksmith-turned-baker. I think my anger was my biggest hurdle."

"I get the impression that your marriage was on shaky ground?"

"About a year and a half after I opened the shop, my wife moved back in with her parents, and I was alone. To keep the bakery running, I sold the house and lived on the premises. I put up a bed in the backroom, so then I both lived and worked there. I was never home anyway, so I might as well sleep there."

"So, now you had eliminated the possibility to get a breath of fresh air or think about something else…because you wanted this that much?"

"Yes, and that was probably too much, because my friends started pulling away from me because I was unpredictable."

"What about your mom, was she still alive?"

"My mom was still alive, but she was a shadow of herself. A year after my wife moved out, my mom moved in with my brother who owned a small house some distance from our town. He was living with his wife and their two kids, and they took care of our mom. My brother is actually one of the people who understands me the best. He remembers that the pressure of taking over the family business fell to me when he got the chance to pursue the job he wanted to do. He's glad that I waited until our dad was dead because he thinks it very well could've killed him. And even though he doesn't necessarily think I'm doing the smartest thing, he understands me. He knows that this is something I've wanted for many years. He tells me that I'm very stubborn but that my stubbornness can be my downfall. That I can't see, or admit to myself, when enough is enough. But he took care of my mom, and my wife had moved back in with her parents, so I was free to go all the way. I was not responsible for my wife, and we never had kids, so I couldn't do any more damage than I had already done. So, I walked the plank."

"How old were you?"

"About 31 years old. The end is kind of a blur."

"In what way?"

"I discovered brandy, and it numbed my anger, but when I drank too much, it became hard to tell friends from foes, so

I let loose on everyone who came into the bakery. Long story short, the more I drank, the fewer customers I had."

"How many years passed while you used brandy to solve your problems?"

"Actually, it lasted for a surprisingly short amount of time compared to how many years it takes other people to bring themselves to ruin. I think it lasted for about a year."

"Did you still have the bakery?"

"It was in foreclosure, and I decided to 'celebrate' with a nice, big bottle of brandy. It was winter, and when I got out into the courtyard to throw out the trash, I fell. I laid there for a while to recover, but before I knew it, I fell asleep and died of the cold. Nobody found me until the next morning."

"Did death come as a relief?"

"No, it was not a relief because I still had something to finish. I have to find out how you rouse people from their own mindlessness, how to give them a good shake or get them to wake up and make conscious decisions in some other way. So, I told the people who had come to pick me up that I was not ready to leave. I spent a while walking around, trying to shake some sense into people, and one day, I met Søren standing in his store, his energy similar to my own, looking out at all the people mindlessly following their old patterns. They headed straight for the next store without so much as stopping to see what his store had to offer."

"So, you saw him standing there, just like you did in your own store?"

"Yes, and I can feel that he feels the same way as me – that people follow the crowd without thinking for themselves. I spend a lot of time in his store trying to wake people up, but my frustration only grows, and Søren's does too. I rush out to people who walk straight past the store and try to get their attention. 'Break the mould and stop following the crowd – there's a man with his life's work and a vision right here, and he has something to offer', I tell them, but they still choose to stick to their habits."

Wake Them Up for Real

"So, you're still very mad?"

"Yes, and I don't know if it's a bad or a good thing. Sometimes when you're mad, you're mad at the whole world. And sometimes you don't even want to leave your anger behind because you aren't done with it."

"Do you think you're reaching a stage where you can let go of your anger?"

"After our conversation today, I can feel that I'm not as angry. Maybe I'm just curious as to why people act the way they do. Why do we continue down a path that doesn't necessarily make sense, and why does it take so much effort to choose a different one, even if it has much more to offer than the one we're on? I guess I'll never understand."

"Maybe it's not about understanding it but accepting it and figuring out how to get through to the people you really 'want' to get through to. When you try to shout sense into people, you tend to cause a disturbance, and that makes them shy away from you and want you to leave. But if you can wake them up, you have their attention, because their eyes are open."

"I can see that it didn't work out when I tried to shout sense into them…Now I understand that people need to be woken up in a different way if you want them to be more conscious about the choices they make."

"In my experience, you can only wake people up if they want to be woken up. If they want to change the path they're on – or the life they lead – then you have their attention."

"Of course, but I also think that things like natural disasters can make people pause and think about what really matters to them in life. Sometimes it isn't until disaster strikes that people realise that what they thought was important doesn't really matter in the big picture. Unfortunately, I think that people need to be shaken to the core before they take a moment to look at their lives."

"There's a fine line between shaking and scaring people, but I see what you mean," Laurens says. "How are you feeling?"

"I'm tired, and I can feel that our talk has given me a little more insight. I think I'm trapped in my own anger, and it's been hard to wake people up with that sidekick, because who wants to listen to anger? The people who are angry but not the people who want to be woken up."

"Someone has come for you…"

A close friend from the afterlife comes into the room. The baker looks at him calmly and signals that he's ready to leave. Laurens looks at the baker and says:

"When I decided to change industry and start working with people, I had a tendency to think like you and focus on what I didn't have. But I discovered that my frustration was a roadblock to the opportunities. You forget what's yet to come and what you're in the middle of creating. I think it's all about setting a good example for yourself. You need to live the life that you think is right, a life that you yourself commend.

That's the only way to appeal to people and inspire them to consider the fact that they can do something different."

The guide looks at Laurens before turning to the baker.

"You've been here for many years. Are you ready to move on?"

"Yes, I am. There's just one thing I'd like to know. I've seen how difficult it is for some people to move on from here, to cross over into the next life. Why is that?" the baker asks.

"Over the course of your life, you have to figure out your feelings, find out what makes you happy and what's good for you, and reach out to people who can help if you can't figure it all out yourself. If you do that, then your transition from life to the afterlife will be nice and easy…" the guide says. "But if you're carrying around heavy baggage, whether that's grief, grudges, hatred, anger, and the things you never said out loud for whatever reason, you won't just have a hard life, but you'll also struggle to cross over into the afterlife. That's what makes you stick around as a ghost."

"It's hard when the things that make you happy, and the things you create, are associated with this desire to be recognised. Maybe the best way to make yourself happy is to create for your own sake rather than for the sake of the people around you. That way, you can inspire others," Laurens says. "Is there anything else you want to say before you head off?"

"I regret making life so difficult for the people closest to me because I was so angry and harboured so much pent-up frustration."

"Nobody holds grudges in the afterlife. Making mistakes is part of your development, and if you learn from your mistakes and fix them, you grow as a person and as a soul," the guide explains.

"Thank you for coming out to tell us about your mission to wake people up," Laurens says.

The baker smiles.

"Thank you for talking to me," he says and looks at Søren. "Good luck with your project, Søren. I hope it works out for you."

The guide and the baker walk out of the room and fade from view. Laurens looks at Søren.

"How are you feeling?"

"The baker was right. I'm carrying around too much frustration to allow me to get people's attention, and I have to do something about that."

Chapter 5
Jokum's Dream
Remember Your Box of Wishes

A family from southern Zealand realise that something is wrong when their pregnant 22-year-old daughter Louise moves back home for a while. Louise's life is a mess, and she's not sure whether she should get an abortion. Her mom doesn't have a lot of energy to spare, seeing as she's been on her own with five kids for years. But one day, Pernille and Laurens come to visit, and that results in a conversation with a ghost that provides some clarity.

"Who are you?"

"I'm the voice of reason," the voice answers very clearly.

"The voice of reason? What do you mean by that?"

"I'm here to share my story with Louise. I've been following her for a while now, and there's something I'd like to tell her." The ghost walks over to Louise and stands close to her.

Louise starts crying.

"It's cold to my right," she says.

"I'm sorry if I've scared you. I don't mean to," the ghost says.

"You look pretty worn. How old are you?" Laurens asks.

"I know, I must look about a decade older than I actually am. I'm 46."

"How long have you been with Louise, and why?"

"I've been following Louise around for a month and a half. I see something in her that reminds me of myself and my experiences. We have the same energy."

"Can you tell me a little bit about yourself, maybe including your name?"

"If you absolutely need to know, it's Jokum."

"Where were you born?"

"I was born in 1917 on a farm on the outskirts of Randers. I'm the oldest of five siblings; after me, my parents had three girls and one boy."

"What did your parents do?"

"My mom took care of the house and the kids, and my dad was a farmer."

"Did he work on the farm you lived on?"

"Yes, my parents owned the farm, and we kept cows, pigs, chickens, and so on, so there's a lot to do."

"Did you get to go to school?"

"Yes, for seven years, and then I helped my dad on the farm. I had been doing that after school and during school vacations for as long as I can remember. I've been helping out since I was a young boy."

"What was your experience of going to school?"

"It was fine. I think I was pretty good at most things. I did my homework, and I made it through the grade system."

"What about the years after school, what were they like?"

"I helped out on the farm on a full-time basis. I was the first person up, and I was the last to sleep. When I was around 14 years old, my dad had an accident and broke something in his back. So, he hunched over when he stood, and he had severe pains in his legs and the small of his back, so I had to start helping out even more."

"Did your dad get better?"

"About a year after the accident, my parents called on me and asked me to come into the living room. My dad hadn't been able to work for the past couple of weeks, and he had a hard time standing up, so I was worried about what they wanted to tell me. When I came into the room, all of my siblings were already at the table, and it felt like all eyes were on me."

"Then what happened?"

"My dad told me that he no longer had the energy to tend to the farm and that we couldn't afford to hire a hand, so if we were going to survive, I had to take over responsibility of the farm and the animals. In other words, I was the one who had to provide for the family from then on."

"Oh, wow. What did you think when he said that?"

"I can feel that something broke inside me." Jokum sighs deeply and continues. "For the longest time, I had been walking around with this dream of seeing the world. I thought maybe I'd like to sail because I had never tried sailing…" Jokum pauses.

"What did you say to your parents?"

"What was there for me to say? They were all sitting there, looking at me, and I could feel the weight of the responsibility…Of course, I told them that I would."

"How old were you at that point?"

"I had just turned 15."

Slaving Away on the Farm

"What happened in the time that followed?"

"I worked hard from sunrise to sunset, if not even later. My dad's condition deteriorated quickly, and I had to take on more and more tasks as time went on. He spent most of the day sitting in his rocking chair, staring blankly into nothing. It was a sorry sight because he had always been a very proud man."

"It was probably hard for him to accept that he could no longer support his family and that he had to hand the responsibility over to his young son."

"I think so too."

"What happened next?"

"My dad died of a lung infection during a particularly bitter winter just shy of three years later. It was a big loss for all of us, my mom especially."

"What was your mom like?"

"She was a thin and somewhat delicate woman, but she was very compassionate. She took care of the home, and I take care of everything outside it."

"What about your siblings? How old were they?"

"My oldest sister was two years younger than me, the next was three years younger, and the youngest was five years younger, and my brother was seven years younger than me."

"Did they help you out?"

Jokum falls quiet for a bit before answering.

"Not particularly. My sister helped my mom with the housework, and my brother watched the chickens, but…I took care of the farm and the animals."

"How did you feel about that?"

Jokum sighs deeply.

"I stuck it out when things got hard because I assumed the others would start lending a hand when they got a little older."

"But that didn't happen?"

"No, because as soon as they were old enough to do it, they moved away from home. My sisters became maids, and my brother…he went sailing."

"So, after a few years, only you and your mom were left on the farm?"

"Yes, but that didn't last long. One day, my oldest sister showed up at the door, suitcase in hand and her son in her arms. Her husband had left her."

"So, she moved back in?"

"Yes."

"How long did she stay for?"

"A number of years."

"What was it like being on the farm together?"

"Things were fine. We adapted, and it was almost like I had a family of my own. Her son called me dad even though he knew that I was not his dad, but I was like a father to him. My sister helped my mom with the cooking, laundry, and all that sort of stuff. It came as a great relief to my mom who had been a little tired, and she was glad that there was life in the house again…I spent most of the days outside, but I thought it was a good and practical solution too."

"Did you never start a family of your own?"

"No, I didn't really have the time or the energy. I woke up early and I went to bed late, and I worked every single day, so I never really got around to courting. In my younger years, I liked the neighbour's daughter, but she moved to Randers and married a man she met in town. I don't think she wanted to spend her entire life on a farm."

"Were you happy with your life?"

"I don't really know. I tried to make the best of the situation and provided for all of us. I guess I had forgotten all about my own hopes and dreams. It's almost as if this life chose what to do with me rather than I chose what to do with it. Things just happened and suddenly that was the way things were, and by that point, it was too late to change it…"

"Right, because that might mean your family losing the farm."

"Probably, yes, and I would not have been able to bear that."

"What happened in the years that followed?"

"My mom died a couple of years later. She died in her sleep after having been under the weather for a while."

"How old were you at this point?"

"I was 41."

"Did your sister and her son still live on the farm?"

"Yes, he had just turned six, and I had a close relationship with him."

"Were you saddened by the loss of your mother?"

"Of course…It was a sad time, but there was still plenty to do, so it didn't take long before life was back to normal, more or less. One day just fed straight into the next." Jokum falls silent for a moment before continuing. "Two years after her death, I got sick myself. I started experiencing awful chest pains, and I coughed up blood. For the first time in my life, I was struggling to complete my tasks and take care of myself."

"What happened? Did you see a doctor?"

"Yes. The doctor told me that I had oesophageal cancer. I didn't want to be hospitalised, because then who would take care of the animals? My sister couldn't do it and my brother was on the other side of the world."

"Then what happened?"

Jokum sighs.

"Shortly after, my sister came home and told me that she had met someone new…She moved in with him with Gustav…my…her son…"

"So, you were alone on the farm again?"

"Yes."

"What happened next? You had been diagnosed with a serious illness, did someone come to lend a helping hand?"

"What do you think?"

"My guess is no," Laurens answers.

"Correct." Jokum pauses. "I…I ended up having to sell all the animals because I couldn't handle the workload. I don't understand why nobody helped me because I had always been taught that you helped each other. I felt like I had spent most of my life helping my family, but when I needed help, everyone else was too busy with their own lives."

"Then what happened?"

"I died in my bed on the farm, and there was nobody by my side. I think it was because I was worn out."

"How old were you at this point?"

"Just turned 46."

"That was the end of a hard life."

"Yes."

Other People's Needs

"You mentioned earlier on that you saw some similarities between your life and Louise's."

"Yes, you see…All my life, I've been focused on helping other people and prioritising their needs. You could say I've been trained to think of other people's needs before considering my own, and I can see that Louise is walking around with the same little box that I have."

"Little box?"

"Yes, Louise has a little box inside. A box where she hides away her hopes and dreams, but it's dusty, and my guess is that she's forgotten it's there."

Louise starts to cry.

Jokum looks over at Louise.

"Can you feel that the things I'm saying are striking a chord inside you?"

Louise nods and continues to cry.

"You've been trained to tend to other people's needs as well, and you've probably been told that it was your responsibility to watch your younger siblings. You're struggling to check in with your hopes and dreams because they're constantly getting pushed aside by external events and demands. Now you have the chance to reach for your dreams for the first time, and what happens? You get pregnant, and once again, you find yourself having to take care of other people and deprioritise yourself."

Louise sits on the end of the couch, sobbing, and Pernille and Laurens decide to take a short break and give Louise the time to compose herself.

After the break, Laurens asks Louise about her dreams.

"What are these dreams that Jokum is talking about?"

Louise sniffles and answers, "Before I got pregnant, I'd decided to start a degree. I applied this summer." The tears double down. Louise continues, "Jokum is spot on. I've always had to do and be a lot of things for other people, my siblings especially. As soon as I would get home from school, my stepdad would tell me to watch my siblings. We'd be told to go to the playground and stay out until dinnertime. It was never about me or what I wanted. And then when I finally decide to pursue a degree, I get pregnant."

"What about your boyfriend or the child's father? Does he support you?" Laurens asks.

"Not exactly, no. We're not dating anymore, and he's started threatening to take the child as soon as it's born because he wants it to live with him." Louise sniffles. "That's almost the worst part. I'd be able to manage the baby, but the thought of having a connection with the father for many years to come makes me feel a little sick."

"Have you considered not keeping the child?" Jokum asks. "I've been following you around lately to encourage you to take responsibility for your life and to choose the life you want…If you don't make a decision, life and your circumstances do it for you, and you might not like the outcome. Do you follow me?"

"Yes," Louise answers and falls quiet. "Definitely…"

"I'm not saying you 'should' get an abortion; I just want you to consider all the options. You have a tendency to follow the crowd, but you're at a crossroads. This is one of the most important moments in your life, and you need to decide what's going to happen. Right now, you're acting like your mom – as if you have no choice or say in the matter," Jokum says.

Be Open to Opportunities

"Let's discuss all the options," Laurens suggests. "What would happen if you had an abortion? Tell me the first thing that pops into your head, Louise."

"My grandma would be awfully disappointed."

"So, if you were to have the baby, it wouldn't necessarily be because you want it but because you're scared of disappointing your grandma or other family members? You're putting other people's needs before your own again," Jokum says.

"I don't know; I'm so confused," Louise answers.

"That's because you've forgotten about your box of wishes. You don't take the time to figure out what you want, and you get all the answers from around you. Find them inside yourself. Spend some time alone. Go for a walk, sit on a bench, and look at the ducks in the pond. Slowly, very slowly, you'll start to realise what feels right to you," Jokum says. "Souls choose their parents themselves, and your child's soul understands that it might not be chosen. But you can also choose to have the child. What are your thoughts on that idea?"

"That it might be hard to find the time and energy to pursue a degree, especially if I have to do it alone," Louise answers.

"I think it's doable, but it means that you need to start prioritising yourself and your needs to a much bigger degree than you've been used to. Of course, it would be all about your kid for the first long time, as it should be, but don't forget about your own life after your maternity leave. Do you see what I'm saying?" Jokum asks.

"Yes, I can already feel that it'd be difficult for me to keep sight of my own hopes and dreams."

"That's something you can work on. When you start spending more time alone, you make the right decisions. Because you're allowed to make a decision here. You know that, right?" Jokum asks.

Louise looks down at her hands in her lap.

"I guess I'm not used to that. I usually do and say whatever other people do."

"Jokum, can I ask you a question?" Laurens asks.

"Of course."

"Why have you stuck around for so long after your death?"

"It's hard to get through to people because they're so preoccupied. But then I met Louise, and she reacted to me. And I finally understood my life story and knew how to pass it on."

"I sense that someone's here for you. Is there anything you'd like to say before you leave?"

Jokum looks over at Louise.

"I know that it's not an easy decision. I didn't manage to stand up for myself and choose myself, but I hope that you do."

"Thank you. I'll always remember your story because if I don't make a decision, it could become mine too," Louise answers.

"A spirit guide has come to pick you up…" Laurens says and steps aside.

"It's a good thing you got the chance to tell your story and that your hard life could do some good in the end, Jokum. I could see the grief leaving your body, and you can rest easy knowing that your experiences were not for nothing because now you've told Louise about them," the guide says.

Jokum smiles.

"I'm tired. Should we leave?"

Jokum smiles and leaves the room with the guide, and as they walk, they fade from view.

Chapter 6
Karl's Compassion
Put Out Your Own Fire First

Camilla from Næstved is a 26-year-old single mom with two children, ages 3 and 1.5. She's been sensing a strange, heavy energy in her apartment for a while, but she's put it down to having too much on her plate. But one day, she feels the heaviness again, and her oldest boy asks, "What's the man doing here?" And she realises that there's someone in the apartment. That turns into a conversation about carrying heavy burdens and shifting focus from other people's problems to your own, so you can release new energy.

Pernille and Laurens haven't been in Camilla's apartment for long before they sense an extremely heavy energy in the kids' playroom.

"Are your children typical?" Pernille asks Camilla in the playroom.

Camilla shakes her head.

"No." She sighs deeply, on the brink of tears.

"That's what I thought – I sense that there's a child with special needs of some sorts," Pernille says.

"Both of them." The tears roll down her cheeks, but Camilla continues, "They have learning difficulties."

"So, you're going through a time with lots of worries?" Laurens asks.

Camilla nods and tries to keep herself together. They sit in silence for a long time before Laurens tries to get in touch with the ghost.

"Can I ask who you are?"

"Let's sit here for a while, find some calm in the eye of the hurricane," the voice answers.

"I'm sensing a man – a grandfatherly type. He's very calm," Pernille says. "Can I ask who you are?"

"Yes, you can. My name is Karl."

"Why are you here with Camilla?" Laurens asks.

"I put out fires," Karl answers.

"You put out fires?"

"Yes."

"Are these mental and emotional fires, or are you talking about physical fires in houses?"

"I'm actually a retired firefighter. I've learned to spot chaos from a distance."

"Where were you a firefighter?"

"In Avedøre, a short distance south of Copenhagen."

"How old are you?"

"I'm 72 years old."

"How did you get in touch with Camilla?"

"At the meeting…"

"The meeting?"

"A meeting with the brains."

"I think it was about the kids," Pernille says.

"Was this at a government office or at an institution?" Laurens asks.

"It was at the hospital."

"What were you doing at the hospital?"

"I was walking around, putting out fires."

"How long have you been dead?"

"About a year and a half."

"And then you met Camilla and decided to follow her. What did you think that you might be able to help her with?"

"I could tell that the burden on Camilla's delicate shoulders was far too heavy, and that weighed me down. I could tell that she didn't have a father figure to watch out for her."

Pernille looks at Camilla and asks, "Do you keep in touch with your dad?"

"Yes, but not in a father-daughter way. He's not the fatherly type, but he does try to help me if I ask him to."

"You remind me of my daughter; she tried to be strong for other people's sakes as well," Karl says.

"Tell us about how your daughter was strong for other people's sakes."

"I don't know where to begin…"

"You can start at the point where things begin to go south."

"One day, she came home from school – high school – and told us that she had met this amazing man. He was from England."

"How much older is he?"

"He was ten years older, and he wanted her to travel to England with him. He said that he had lots of money and could create a wonderful life for them. But she had only

102

known him for a short while, around three months, and I didn't like him. It might sound weird, but I think he was too smiley and a little too slick. So, it was a bit of a balancing act. Should I tell her straight up not to do it, or should I try to speak to her senses and let her make the decision for herself? I tried to ask her if maybe she should finish school before leaving, but she took a leave of absence at the end of her second-to-last year and goes with him."

The Bad Feeling

"How did things develop from there?"

"They moved to the south of England, and when I talked to her, she told us all about how happy she is. My wife was proud to say that her daughter had found herself a husband and that they lived in the south of England with all this money and that things were going so well."

"When did you feel like something was wrong for the first time? Before or after she'd moved?"

"After she'd moved."

"Did it take long before you got that feeling?"

"No, looking back on the whole thing, I'd say it almost happened immediately. It was the 1960s and money was tight, so we only called each other once a month."

"Who called who?"

"We call her, but even though she said all the right words, something in her voice had changed. My wife was the kind of person who focused on the words people say, so if our daughter told us that everything was fine that meant that things are fine, whereas I read between the lines, and I had a feeling that something was very wrong."

"Time passes, what happened?"

"Before long, she was pregnant. I think she was too young; she was only 18."

"Did you see her in the time between her moving and her getting pregnant?"

"No, we only talked on the phone, and we agreed that we would come visit her when the child was born. My daughter wanted us to come and help out because her husband travelled a lot for work."

"How did you feel about the idea of seeing her again?"

"I was excited. I was excited to see her and put the weird feeling behind me."

"Did you talk more in the lead up to the birth?"

"Yes, and she always insisted that everything was perfectly fine."

"Did she elaborate or was it more of a stubborn insistence?"

"No, I don't think so; she was just persistent."

"So, one might have assumed that everything was fine, but you had a feeling that that was not the case?"

"I sensed that there was chaos lurking beneath the surface."

"Did she give birth to a boy or a girl?"

"She gave birth to a boy two days before her due date, and the birth passed without any complications. Our tickets were booked for the due date, so we arrived two days after the birth."

"What was it like to see her again?"

"I must admit I cried."

"That's understandable. It had been a long time since you last saw each other, and you had this unsettling uncertainty regarding her wellbeing. And becoming a grandfather is a big change as well. Was she doing okay?"

"She said she was, but there was something in her eyes...A haunted expression."

"How much time did you spend with her?"

"14 days."

"What was that time like?"

"Like a movie."

"A horror movie or a romcom?"

"One of those movies where everything is perfect. Like a romantic family movie like *Thanksgiving*. Things are a little too perfect, a little too decked out."

"Did you get to know her husband a little better?"

"Yes, he seemed really nice, and he had an eye for detail."

"What do you mean by 'detail'?"

"He paid attention to the small things, remembered the tiniest details, and he was incredibly thorough."

"In a neat or a controlling way?"

"At first glance, it seems gentlemanlike and polite, but it was weird. I usually have a pretty good feel for the situation, and even though I couldn't figure out what it was, I still had this feeling that something was not right."

"So, when it was time to leave, you still didn't know where this feeling was coming from. How did you feel?"

"It was a difficult time because I didn't know if...or when I'd see her again."

"Did you feel like it was mostly the question of 'if' you'd see her again?"

"Yes."

"What about the time after you got back home, what was that like?"

"Life went on as normal. We kept calling her every month, and she said the same thing every time we talked together. She thought that having a small child was hard, but otherwise everything was fine."

"Is she your only daughter?"

"Yes."

"Everything continued to be fine, but then a fateful day arrived. Tell us what happened."

The Blow to the Perfectionist

"One day, she called to tell us that the child's speech had suddenly stopped developing and that he needed to go in for testing. It turned out that he had an illness that would make him go deaf by the age of five."

"Did the illness break him down completely, or did it only affect his hearing?"

"Only his hearing, and my daughter took it like a champ and immediately signed up for a sign language class."

"How did you and your wife take the news?"

"Fine, it just meant that we had to take a class as well. But shortly after that, I started getting more and more worried. My daughter slowly opened up and told us that her husband was having a hard time with the fact that their child was hearing impaired."

"Did he take it personally, or was it just the circumstances?"

"My perception of him is that he was a perfectionist, and this hurdle doesn't fit into his world of straight lines and attention to detail. This was a thing that wasn't perfect and that he couldn't control, so things between my daughter and him took a turn for the worse. But whenever we asked her about it, she told us not to worry. That they were just going through a hard time."

"Tell us more about this difficult period."

"A year and a half go by, and we saw them once after the child had been declared deaf. We had taken a sign language class before going to see them, but when we get over there, we discover that the Danish and English sign language systems are slightly different, so it was hard to talk to our grandchild. The sight of our daughter almost scared us. Her energy was completely different, and she seemed haunted and was always on edge…Her smile seemed very artificial."

"What did you make of her physical condition?"

"Everything looked fairly normal from the outside. She might have lost a little weight, but she kept saying, 'Stop it, Daddy,' because that's what she called me, 'I'm fine, and I'll make it through this.' I pulled her aside and asked about her marriage in a way that only a worried father could, but I got the same answer: 'Don't worry, Daddy, my husband is just going through a rough patch, but things will turn around.' That's the last time I saw her."

"I can feel that it weighs you down, but try to tell us a little more about what happened, if you can."

Karl sighs and continues.

The Murder

"We get a call one Sunday morning and found out that she was dead. She'd broken her neck after falling down a flight of stairs."

"When did you last see her?"

"Eight months before her death."

"You had been walking around with that sense of uncertainty for so many years, and now your worst fear had come true. What was the first thought that crossed your mind?"

"That he was responsible. He was arrested for the murder of my daughter."

"How did that play out?"

"In the beginning, he denied it. He claimed that it was an accident, that she fell down the stairs with a bag she was carrying, but when they examine her body, they find a series of old fractures that made them suspicious. He ended up admitting that they had a fight, and as she backed away from him, she fell down the stairs by accident. I wish she would've told us what was going on in their home, and I would've come to get her immediately."

"For some reason, she didn't want to show you any sign of weakness. She didn't want to show you that she was failing. Why do you think she didn't say anything to you, of all people? You were her 'daddy' after all."

"We had always been proud of her. We had always praised her for being so talented and being good at so many things. Maybe it was because she wanted to prove that she could do it herself. Maybe she found it hard to accept that things weren't working out too. I mean, we did tell her that it might be better to wait and that she didn't know him very well when she left and all that. I guess she didn't want to tell us that we were right...But I don't know."

"What was your daughter's relationship with her mom like?"

"It was fine; I don't think there were any problems between them. I had always felt like they had a good relationship."

"I understand her holding back when it came to saying this difficult thing, because you're her 'daddy', and she's too proud, but I don't understand her never letting her guard down to admit that things were really bad. I know that it's hard to balance fending for yourself with finding out what that entails, because when should you deal with it yourself and when should you reach out to your mom or dad?"

"She was only 24 years old."

"So, asking for help wasn't her forte. Are you good at asking for help?"

"I don't know; I've never thought about it."

"I'm wondering whether you've been good at putting out fires in your own life. You do it for other people, and you've spent your whole life doing it. I'm thinking you must have considered it a passion – a calling, even."

"The irony is that I've put out so many fires and saved so many people...but the only person I couldn't save was my own daughter. But that was because I could only see the smoke and never the flames."

"Exactly, and when it comes to Camilla, I assume you'd like to put out her fire because there's more than just smoke. There are flames everywhere."

"Yes, and she's dealing with it all alone."

"I think Camilla needs help from someone she can bounce her ideas off, but I think she needs to do that with someone who can put out their own fires. Someone who has the right experience, emotionally speaking."

"What do you mean?" Karl asks.

"It's great of you to want to help Camilla and be there to support her. It's coming from a good place, but when you attach yourself to Camilla, she gets attached to someone who's really good at putting out other people's fires, whereas what she needs is someone who can teach her how to stop focusing on putting out other people's fires and start putting out her own."

"Right," Karl nods. "I just thought that seeing as I couldn't save my own daughter, I might be able to help someone else's, especially if her parents didn't know the burdens she was walking around with. That's why I followed Camilla home."

Focus on the Important Things

"You've been a massive help because the fact that you were following Camilla around made her contact us, and as a result, we now have an insight into a life, into your story of putting out other people's fires. We spend a lot of time working with people, inspiring and teaching them to put out their own fires first. If we do that, it's easier to tell whether we need to put out theirs at all. Your presence has brought attention to what Camilla needs to focus on going forward... You've highlighted the issue, but maybe you're not the one who needs to help her, so I'm thinking it might be time for someone else to take over. What do you say?" Laurens asks.

"What does Camilla say?" Karl asks.

"I don't know what to say. What does that mean?"

"It means that you can always turn to Pernille or me for example. We have experience working with people, and we can give you some valuable tools to help you put out your own fires first. That's what I think you need," Laurens answers.

"I would love that."

"What do you say, Karl?" Laurens asks.

Karl looks at Camilla.

"Is there anything in my story that strikes a chord with you, Camilla? Something that has got you thinking?"

"I think I'm good at unloading, but I find it hard to open up and talk about what's actually happening in my life. But I'm working on that."

"This idea of saying that everything is under control even though nothing is, and everything is actually chaos, is that something you recognise?"

"I can see that that's how I act on a daily basis, but I only feel like I do that when I'm talking to people I don't know."

"Do you do that with your dad?"

"More so with him than with other people, I guess. He doesn't ask about the emotional side of things, so he doesn't know much about how I'm feeling. He's very physical and practical, so it's hard to talk feelings with him."

"How would he react if you were to say: 'Dad, it's all gone belly-up, can you help me'?"

"He wouldn't be able to help me."

"So, you'd be left to fend for yourself?"

"Yes."

"What about your burdens? Who needs to deal with those?" Karl asks.

"I suppose I have to do that myself."

"I can see that you're carrying around too much weight and issues too big for your own good. Something in your life has gotten better, but there's still something you're dreading."

111

"Karl, you've been following Camilla around for a while. Is there anything you can point out that she can't see for herself?" Laurens asks.

Karl turns to Camilla.

"You have a beautiful soul and a good heart, but you have a tendency to deprioritise your own needs. I'm worried that these burdens will drain you so much, you'll lose the will to live. I see you slowly putting out your happiness and your love for yourself, all the while thinking that things are bound to turn around soon. When will you pause or get the chance to pause? To take in the sunshine or hear the birdsong? It's almost like you're living by this idea that things are better when you're having a hard time."

"I sense that Camilla does more than just remind you of your daughter and the chance to make things right. She also stirs up a sense of grief."

"You're right...It's never fun to lose your daughter..."

"Karl, do you have any advice for Camilla?"

"Yes. Remember that you're allowed to focus on yourself, and that's true even though you have kids with special needs...And you're allowed to live your life, set your worries aside, and have a good time. There's too much mothering and thinking about what you can do for other people and not enough 'you'."

"You said that the last time you saw your daughter was when you left England back then. Am I right in thinking that you haven't seen her since?"

"Yes."

Laurens steps to the side, and in comes Karl's daughter. She's come to pick Karl up. She rolls her eyes and says, "Dad,

I thought you had learned that you shouldn't help people who haven't asked for help."

Karl gets a little emotional.

"But I feel like Camilla did ask for help."

Laurens looks at Camilla and asks, "Have you ever sat here and thought: 'I wish someone would come and help me'?"

"Many times, I think."

"Do you have anyone who can help you with what's to come?" Karl asks.

"I have the people already in my life, and then I have Pernille and Laurens if I need them."

"Okay, that's good to hear."

"I'd like to thank you for coming and bringing Camilla's attention to the fact that there are plenty of opportunities in her life, if only she'd stop and look around. You've also pointed out that whatever you think, that's what you attract and what you create. That's a really strong message. I can see that your daughter's pulling you away, so it's probably time to go."

"I hope I haven't scared you, Camilla. That was never my intention. I just wanted to help," Karl says. "My daughter's telling me to come with her now."

Karl and his daughter leave the room, and as they walk, they fade away.

"How do you feel?" Laurens asks Camilla.

"Weird but okay."

"Good, but I do think you need to give yourself some time to process all of this. After all, the heavy energy in your home didn't come from the fact that Karl wanted to help you but rather from the grief of having lost his daughter and the guilt of not having done better – not having been able to save her. It might have been easier for him to leave this life if he hadn't been so weighed down, if he'd put out his own fire instead of ignoring it by trying to put out other people's. So, what do you need to remember going forward?"

"To fix my own problems before trying to fix other people's," Camilla answers.

Chapter 7
Jakob's Fatal Game
We're Not as Alone as We Think

In a cosmetic store north of Copenhagen, there's a basement with a safe. When the manager, Kirsten, brings the cash take down to the safe at the end of each day, she finds herself feeling sad. And the sadness grows with every passing day. It confuses her because there's nothing in her life weighing her down. But one day, a little boy in pyjamas appears. The story he shares strikes a chord and serves as evidence that we're never as alone as our thoughts make us think we are.

Kirsten, Pernille, and Laurens sit down on the basement floor.

"Can I ask who you are?" Laurens begins.

"I'm Jakob."

"You don't look very old."

Jakob looks around shyly.

"I'm only six."

"What are you doing down here?"

"I'm hiding."

"Who or what are you hiding from?"

"When it started snowing, I walked around to find a place to hide. There was an open trapdoor leading down here, so I crawled in for the night. I didn't think anything of it. I was very scared."

"So, it wasn't because you were looking for something special?"

"No, I was trying to get away. I was trying to hide."

"What were you trying to get away from?"

"I just had to get away from the adults, away from the staff. I was scared that they would put me in jail. I've heard that kids can go to prison too."

"Why are they after you, and why do you think they want to put you in jail?"

"I killed Karl."

"Who's Karl?"

"He was my best friend."

"How did you meet Karl?"

"I met him at the orphanage. He was already there when we get dropped off."

"You say that you, plural, got dropped off. Who do you mean?"

"Me and my little sister."

"How old was she when you got dropped off at the orphanage?"

"She was not even three years old yet."

"And how old were you at the time?"

"Almost six."

"Is Karl older, or were you around the same age?"

"He was half a year older than me. We quickly became friends, and the others say we were like the same person."

"In what way? Did you look alike or was it because you acted the same?"

"I had brown hair, and Karl was blond, so it must be because we acted the same."

"Was Karl your first close friend?"

"No, I'd had other close friends. When we lived with my mom, we played with the other kids in the courtyard, but things were different at an orphanage when you spent all your time together. Karl and I practically became brothers because we spent every waking moment together."

"You mentioned the courtyard and your mom. Where did you live?"

"I don't know."

"But it was a building with multiple floors?"

"Yes, and we played with the other kids on the big field."

"Is that where you were born?"

"Yes."

"Were your mom and dad together?"

"Yes."

"What did your dad do?"

"I don't know; I was very young, but I do remember that he was gone for long periods of time. We spent a lot of time waiting for my dad."

"Did you wait for days or even weeks?"

Jakob nods.

"Then I think he might have been a fisherman."

"Do you remember anything about your childhood before your sister was born?"

"Yes, I played, and my mom often sang to me."

"Was she a good singer?"

"I think so, yeah."

"And then your mom got pregnant?"

"Yeah, and then my little sister arrived. She was so lovely; she looked like an angel when she was born. Her hair was all white."

"So, you were happy when she arrived. Had you been looking forward to it?"

Jakob nods.

"Yes, very much so."

"Was your sister normal, so to speak?"

"Yeah, she was just fine."

"What was life like at home after your sister arrived? Did you help out, or did you still play with your friends in the courtyard?"

"I remember spending a lot of time in the courtyard with my mom sitting on one of the benches with the other moms, watching my sister in the baby carriage. My mom talked a lot to the other moms. I think she was very happy."

"How was your dad?"

"He was not at home a lot. I didn't know him that well." In an embarrassed whisper, Jakob continues, "I don't actually remember my dad's name."

"That's nothing to be embarrassed about. It's not your fault that he's never home and doesn't want to spend time with you, your mom, or your sister. There's a reason kids often try to make their own rules about what they are and aren't allowed to do and how life should be when their parents aren't around to help them."

"My mom took good care of me."

"I'm sure she did, but were you starting school soon?"

"Yes, the following summer, but then my mom got sick."

"How old were you when your mom got sick?"

"Five."

"What was wrong with her?"

"She had cancer."

"How did that affect your life at home? Did your dad stop fishing and come back?"

"I never saw him again. My mom kept telling me that he might be coming home, but he never did, and then my mom went to the hospital to have surgery, so the neighbour, who has three kids, watched us. We stayed there for a whole week because there was no one else to take care of us."

"How old were the neighbour's kids? Did you know them well?"

"Yeah, they were the kids I played with down in the courtyard. There was also a really young one. I didn't know her. My mom told us to be good and not make life harder for Mrs Hansen."

"How were things at the neighbour's place?"

"We were on our best behaviour; I promised mom that much."

"What happened after that week?"

"My mom came home, but we ate at Mrs Hansen's place most nights, and my mom slept a lot. I was scared that something would happen to her; she seemed really tired. She smiled when we went into her bedroom, but sometimes she didn't have the energy to hold my hand."

"Were you scared that she was going to die?"

"Yes."

"What did your mom tell you?"

"She told me to be strong and brave and that she would hold on for as long as she can, and then she told me to take good care of my little sister if she gets so sick that she doesn't wake up again."

"What's your little sister's name?"

"Sofie Amalie."

"Did you tell your mom that you'd take care of her, or did you think it?"

"I promised her that I'd take care of my sister the best I knew how."

The Orphanage

"How long did she stick it out for?"

"I'm not sure, but I think it was around six months. She was very pale, and she got taken to the hospital many times, so we lived with Mrs Hansen. One day, Mrs Hansen came home and said…that Mommy was not coming home again."

"What happened inside you when you heard that?"

"I cried because I loved my mom."

"How did your younger sister take it? Was she there when you got the news?"

"Yeah, she was there. Mrs Hansen walked into the living room and sent the other kids out, and then she squatted down in front of us and said that Mommy wasn't here anymore…and that she wouldn't be coming home again…My sister, Fie, asked if we could live with Mrs Hansen."

"What did Mrs Hansen say in response?"

"She said that she didn't know if we could, that it was not up to her…When we had said goodbye to Mommy and put flowers on her grave, a woman in a skirt and a blazer came to pick us up."

"Were you being told what was happening? Did Mrs Hansen say anything?"

"I don't really remember. We didn't talk much. We didn't play much anymore either." Jakob falls silent.

"I don't blame you for being quiet given all the emotions that must have been in play with the recent chain of events."

"I took care of my sister, and she spent a lot of time with me. She missed Mommy too. The lady brought us into a big room with a table in the middle and told us that we were going to move somewhere where there were other kids who have lost their mommy and daddy…She told us that we'd wait there while they tried to find us a new mommy and daddy…We wanted a new mommy and daddy. It was hard to not have a mommy or a daddy…especially when you don't have a mommy. I told the woman that Daddy might be coming home, but she just kept talking about other things. So, we went to the place where there were other kids who didn't have a mommy or a daddy."

"Was it far from where you used to live?"

"I don't know…We rode in a car, and it was the first time I was inside a car, so it was very exciting."

"So, you didn't think about how far you drove?"

"No…I only had a bike…and it's easy to go far in a car, much easier than on a bike. When we got to the big house, I was a little shy because everyone was looking at us. I was holding Fie's hand, and she had her teddy with her."

"So, you felt a little bit stronger when you were holding each other's hands."

"Yeah, I had to take care of her…I promised Mommy I would. The lady brought us inside, and there was another lady waiting. She looked a little strict."

"Was she the matron?"

"I think that was her title. She showed us around, so we could meet the other kids."

"Were there a lot of children?"

"How many is a lot?"

"Do you think there was a lot?"

"Yeah, I think there were a lot of kids…and that was when I noticed Karl. He winked at me."

"It was almost like he had been waiting for you?"

"It was like he wanted to be my friend, so that made me happy. It was nice to have new friends when you moved somewhere new. But it was hard to sleep at night because there were lots of kids crying, and I missed my mommy and daddy most at night. That was when I realise that I was not a big boy – it was easier to be a big boy when the sun was out because then you could play and do other things. We went to school and had lessons during the day, and I looked forward to that."

"What was it like trying to settle into the orphanage?"

"There were a lot of rules, but I understood why. It was important to wash up and brush your teeth. We had to do a lot of things ourselves because there weren't as many grownups as there were kids, but it was nice to have a close friend. That made life easier."

"How about Fie? Did she have an easy time following the rules too?"

"Yeah, Fie was allowed to do all sorts of things; everyone loved Fie. She was not that old, not even three, and she was so pretty. She had long, blonde hair with a nice bow in it, and she spent a lot of time sitting with the grownups. Otherwise, she was with me."

"What about you and Karl, did you pull pranks?"

"No, we played tag, hide and seek, and baseball if we were outside."

"What did you talk about?"

"We talked about what our new mommy and daddy were going to look like. We tried to be on our best behaviour, so the new grownups would like us. Once in a while, the ones who wanted to take a kid home came to look at us. So, we made sure to comb our hair and put on our Sunday best."

"And cleaned your nails…"

Jakob smiles.

"Yeah, almost always."

"Did they always pick the pretty kids?"

"The youngest kids."

"How old were the kids at the orphanage?"

"You could stay there as soon as you were born and until…I don't really know…but some of them were a little older than me, a couple of years older."

"What about Karl, did he go to school too?"

"Even though he was a half a year older than me, we were going to start together. We spent a lot of time talking about who might want us…Karl had been there longer than I had."

"What happened to Karl's mom and dad?"

"I think they were both dead."

"Did Karl have any siblings?"

"No, he was an only child, and he'd been at the orphanage for a while. He wasn't even two years old when he arrived."

"So, Karl knew all about life at the orphanage, and I assume that was an advantage for you. He knew the rules and the loopholes, and that must have been helpful for you, so you could take good care of Fie and yourself."

"Sometimes he was sad because he looked at a lot of parents, but not that many have looked at him. I don't know why that is because I think he was a really good friend. We hoped that we could end up together…Karl, Fie, and me."

"But destiny had other things in store?"

Jakob nods.

The Pretty Couple

"This pretty couple came. The woman smelled like perfume, and she told Fie that she was adorable. I remember that clear as day. I stood next to my sister, but the woman didn't say that I was adorable. Then she picked up Fie and put her on her lap. Fie smiled like Fie always did with her big, blue eyes, and her long, blonde hair still had the pretty bow in it. I tied the bow for her. Maybe I shouldn't have…The pretty couple with the perfume talked to the grownups for a while, and I knew that it was about Fie. So, they left, and that night, I talked to Fie and told her that I think that man and woman wanted her. She was very happy and said that we were getting a new mommy and daddy. I didn't want to tell her that I just meant her. I didn't think they wanted me. I was not adorable. I didn't sleep a wink that night because I had promised to take care of her. I asked a grownup about the pretty couple, but she was harsh and told me that if that's the case, I should just be happy for Fie because she'll get to go to a nice school and get new shoes and do well…it's better than being at the orphanage."

"How do you take that?"

"I thought it was best for her to stay with me. She was my Fie, and I'd promised Mommy that I would take care of her…so I ended up making trouble."

"How so?"

"I got angry pretty easily, so I ended up hitting one of the other boys who teased me by saying they only wanted Fie and not me. I thought he was really stupid. I got pulled into the office, and they hit me over the fingers with a ruler. And then the door opened, and Karl came in. He was being punished too because he jumped on the boy who was teasing me. So, we sat there waiting, and that happened a couple of times. I thought to myself that my mom would probably be mad."

"Yes, it would be difficult to take care of Fie from in there."

Jakob nods.

"The days passed. How long before the pretty couple came back?"

"It was only a couple of weekends, and then they came to pick up Fie. They'd bought her a neat suitcase for all of her things, and she looked happy. I didn't think she understood that I was not going with her. I stood there with the matron who was holding onto my shoulder. I got to say goodbye, and I started to cry. Then Fie cried too. She didn't say much, but she cried the whole way out."

"She probably didn't understand why you weren't leaving together."

"She sobbed loudly all the way out to the car…and that's the last time I saw her…but I kept thinking about what the grownups said…that she'll go to a good school and get nice shoes."

"Better opportunities, maybe."

125

"Maybe Mommy and Daddy were happy about it."

"How did you feel when they came to pick up Fie?"

"I don't know…I cried on the inside."

"How were the days after that?"

"I waited at the window a lot. I hoped that they would come back to return her, but they didn't."

"What about Karl, how did he feel about it all?"

"He was my best friend. We spent a lot of time talking to each other, and sometimes we didn't talk; we just played. But when we talked, we always dreamed about getting the same mommy and daddy, so we could stay together, and maybe when we're a little older, we could visit Fie."

Jakob continues, "Sometimes I thought about my daddy. Why didn't he come home to get us? But then I told myself that something probably happened to him. That it was not because he didn't want to…Do you think something happened to him?"

Laurens swallows deeply, and a tear rolls down his cheek.

"I think so…I think so…"

"If you had been at the orphanage with me when you were young, we would've had fun. Maybe you would've been hit with the ruler too. That wasn't as fun."

"I think so too. Did you still wait for Fie?"

"Yes…It was almost winter, and I was still waiting, but I also played."

"Then what happened?"

"The awful thing happened…"

"Go on…"

A Dangerous Game

"Karl and I were playing in the big hall at the orphanage where there were a huge staircase up to the first floor. We had come up with a game where we slid down the banister. We had been told many times that it was very dangerous, but one night when we couldn't sleep, we snuck out of the dorm and played hide and seek in the hall. It was kind of exciting. Karl was hiding and I was seeking, and I found him sitting on the banister. I snuck up behind him and said 'Gotcha', but he got so scared that he fell over the banister and down into the hall. I still remember the sound of him hitting the floor…and then I ran."

"Was this in the middle of the night?"

"Yes, it was completely dark, and nobody was awake. I ran down the staircase."

"In your pyjamas?"

"Yeah, and I was not wearing shoes. I opened the big main door and ran outside. Now that I'd done something like that to my best friend, I was sure that no grownup would want me. I was scared that they'd throw me in prison because that's where bad boys go, so I just kept running."

"You just ran away?"

"Yeah, as far away as possible…I also cried a little but not much because I was scared that someone would hear me and catch me. Suddenly, it got really cold, maybe because I was not wearing shoes. I found a trapdoor and thought to myself that I could hide there until they stopped looking for me."

"Was your hiding place warm?"

Jakob shakes his head.

"I think it was very cold."

"Did you go to bed, or did you just fall asleep?"

"I hid…I tried not to sleep."

"But you fell asleep?"

"Yeah."

"Did you wake up?"

"It's weird because I woke up and crawled further in, and then I turned around to see that I was lying there sleeping…and suddenly there were two of me."

"What was your first thought?"

"I thought, 'I wish Mommy was here to explain what's happening because I didn't understand.' But then I thought that she wouldn't be coming to help me because I hadn't taken care of Fie and I just killed my best friend."

"So, you thought that nobody in the world liked you?"

"I was very ashamed, so I hid for a long time every time someone came up until the day I got brave enough to say something to the lady who looked like my mom." Jakob looks over at Kirsten, who's sitting there with tears rolling down her cheeks.

"Did someone find your body in your hiding place?"

"I don't know…I don't think so…I don't remember, but I am in a different place now. But I keep getting braver and braver, and I try to say hi to the woman who looks like my mommy, but she gets sad and rushes out of the room. I don't blame her. I'm a bad boy. I'm kind of sad, but then you came and talked to me today, and I'm glad. But I miss Mommy, Fie, and Karl."

Broken Leg

"Jakob, there's someone here who wants to see you." Laurens steps aside.

Karl appears in the room. He's come to pick up Jakob.

"There you are, Karl…You're walking funny," Jakob says with a hint of uncertainty in his voice. He smiles.

"Well, I did fall into the hall and break my leg and it didn't grow back together right."

"So, you didn't die?"

"No."

"So, you're not mad at me?"

"Not at all. We went looking for you, but we eventually gave up."

"I'm glad you're not mad. Did you ever get a new mommy and daddy?"

"No," Karl answers, "but I got a wife and kids of my own." While he talks about his own family, he changes shape from a child to a grown man.

Jakob looks on, his eyes wide.

"You're a magician, Karl."

Karl smiles.

"Come on, best friend, no need to feel so bad. You're coming with me now. We have so much to talk about, and we have plenty of time to do it. Just you and me."

Jakob smiles and looks at Kirsten.

"Can I go with Karl?"

"Yes, do that," Kirsten replies.

On the way out of the room, Jakob asks Karl if he's seen Fie.

"Yeah, I have. She enrolled in a good school and got the nicest shoes, and she named all her teddy bears Jakob and named her first child Jakob."

"Have you seen my mommy too?" Jakob asks.

"Yes, and she's not mad at you. She's mostly upset that thing ended up the way they did, but you can talk to her yourself soon…they're waiting."

As they leave the room, they fade from view.

Laurens looks at Kirsten.

"How do you feel?"

"I'm fine now. I can feel Jakob's story tugging at my heartstrings. That feeling of being alone in the world, that nobody likes you, I know that all too well. It actually takes up a lot of space in my life, but his story has given me the courage to finally change that."

Chapter 8
Jarl on the Farm
Arbitrary Rules Steal Dreams

Torben has been trying to sell a large, old farm in southern Denmark for a year, but in spite of his many adverts, nobody has shown any interest in the property. Having gone through a turbulent period in his life, including a divorce, Torben is desperate to leave. He decides to get some clarity on the negative energy on the farm which had previously been home to a collective and a religious sect, not to mention a residence for prominent business people. The ghost who has set up shop here loves strict discipline, but Torben teaches him that gentleness can lead to many good things and rekindle old friendships.

When Pernille and Laurens come to visit, the energy on the farm is powerful. The living room boasts an atmosphere of politics, power, and manipulation, while the first floor is teeming with powerlessness and worry. They decide to start in the living room where they sit down on the couch.

"I hear someone saying, 'Join the club'," Laurens says and looks at Pernille.

"It's a man in his late 60s who doesn't want to talk to me. He's looking at you," Pernille says to Torben and Laurens.

"I feel like women don't have access to this room," Laurens says. "He tells me that women are a necessary evil." Laurens talks directly to the ghost. "That might be how you feel about women but try to move past that, so we can talk and hear your story. Who are you?"

"I'm the boss."

"I'm glad because I'd love to talk to the boss. The boss of what?"

"My grandfather had slaves in the Danish West Indies. He ran his own company, and I ran an orphanage for many years."

"Do you have a name aside from 'the boss'?"

"I guess I do, but I'm not interested in telling you right now."

"How old are you?"

"I'm 65...I look good for my age."

"Do you know if you've been dead for a long time?"

"I suppose that's something you realise along the way...when it occurs to you that nobody is answering your questions."

"Do you remember when you realised?"

The ghost is quiet.

"I feel like you've been here for many years."

The ghost answers with some hesitation.

"I like the place. I'm a person with power, and I'm most comfortable being around the people with power, the people who make the decisions."

"Why is it that you don't like women?"

"Back in my day, they didn't have much of a say in anything. They were Mrs Director and Mrs Carpenter. Their only worth was their husband's profession."

"So, you were alive in the 1930s or 40s?"

The ghost nods.

"What was your profession at the time?"

"I was a schoolteacher."

"Had you just started or had that been your profession for a while?"

"I was an experienced teacher, and I ended up having to choose between being a principal or head of an orphanage."

"So, you've spent some years in the education system?"

"Yes, more than 20 years."

"You were in your mid-40s at that point?"

"Yes, but ask me about the decision with the school and the orphanage."

"Which of the two did you choose?"

"I chose the orphanage."

"Why?"

"As a principal, I'd only have the power to influence the kids during the day, but at an orphanage, I had that power round-the-clock."

"Did you exert a good influence on them? Did you get a lot of recognition at the orphanage for the way you ran the place?"

"Nobody slacked at my orphanage. We had a strict culture of discipline."

"But did it win you recognition?"

"In some circles."

"Where did your attitude to influencing kids come from? How had it arisen, and why did you want to influence children?"

"My grandfather always told my father that kids and blacks were less developed, so you had to raise them with tight reins to get a good result."

"Looking at yourself, do you think you're an example of a good result?"

"I think so. It's all about gaining influence and using your influence, making a mark on other people's lives. That's the meaning of life."

"I'm Laurens. What's your name?"

"You can call me Jarl."

"So, you chose the orphanage based on the idea that you could achieve good results by giving the kids tight reins, but where did you grow up?"

"Southern Zealand."

"That must have been in the late 1800s, around the turn of the century?"

"That's about right."

"On a farm or in a town?"

"In a small, but important, town."

"Important in what way? Try to explain."

"It was an important trading hub."

"What about your family? Did you have a lot of siblings?"

"There were eight kids: six boys and two girls."

"What did your dad do?"

"He was a merchant."

"Did he travel a lot?"

"No, he was a shipping coordinator."

"What about your mom? Was she a homemaker?"

"Of course…She was responsible for the family. There were many duties."

"As you got older, did you start helping out at home?"

Jarl looks at Laurens with some confusion.

"It's my belief that the girls help out at home, not the boys."

"How old were the girls compared to the boys?"

"One was the second-to-oldest, the other was the second-to-youngest."

"So, they helped out at home. What did you do?"

"I focused on school."

"How many years were you in school?"

"More than most people…I attended a private school."

"Did all your siblings go to a private school or just the boys?"

"All the boys bar one. He was not that good with his head; he was much better with his hands, so he did an apprenticeship."

"What about your sisters, did they go to school?"

"Yes, but only for six years. They only did the required years."

"How did you do at school?"

"I did well; I'm good at numbers."

"Is there anything you aren't that good at?"

"No."

"So, you were good at everything at school?"

"Where are you going with these questions?"

"I'm wondering if being good at school was important to you because there were things in your life that you weren't that good at, or if it was because you had a goal of being important and successful."

"I had a legacy to live up to."

"Your dad's or your grandfather's?"

"My family's."

The Power of Teaching

"What did the family legacy mean to you?"

"Exerting influence wherever you could, making your mark on the town, on the people."

"What did you do once you were done with school?"

"I became a teacher."

"Did you want to become a teacher, or was there something else that you think you might have wanted to be?"

"I didn't really think about that because my dad thought I would make a great schoolteacher, so I wanted to prove to him that he was right."

"Did any of your brothers end up taking a path other than the one your dad considered the right one?"

"Not really."

"Did all of your brothers make it through school okay?"

"Yeah. Except the one who wasn't right in the head."

"What did he end up doing?"

"Taking care of the animals at a farm."

"Was he happy?"

"I don't know; I didn't see him very often…We didn't have much in common."

"Did you have anything in common with your other brothers?"

"I would argue that we all had big ambitions."

"Did any of them choose the same path as you and become educators?"

"No."

"So, did you and your brothers have anything in common aside from the fact that you had big ambitions?"

"Many of us found history interesting."

"History means many things. Which part did you find interesting?"

"Politics and Danish history in the era where Denmark made its mark. My dad proudly called us his small soldiers of society."

"So, you went out into the world to make your mark and get results."

"I'd say so, yes."

"Did you have a couple of years where you did something else after you left school or did you go straight into the educational system?"

"I took the direct path."

"How long did it take to become a teacher at that time?"

"It differed from person to person. It depended on your contacts and what recommendations you could get."

"So, getting into the right places was all about knowing someone who knows someone."

"I started out teaching math and history."

"How old were you when you finished school?"

"16…" Jarl answers with pride.

"When did you teach for the first time?"

"When I was around 20 years old."

"What was it like standing there in front of all the kids for the first time after everything with school, your dad's expectations of you being successful, and your own goal to prove him right?"

"It was amazing…All that power in the palm of your hand. You walked into the room and the kids stood up. I liked that."

"So, it was a dream come true."

"Yes, I almost felt high from the discipline."

"What was it like to be the one in charge of changing and influencing the direction things went in? Did you have any thoughts about what that power might lead to?"

"I remember the principal at the time telling me that he'd never met someone so young who was so naturally authoritative…And I thought to myself, 'I wonder what this could lead to'."

"So, all of a sudden the world was your oyster?"

"Yes, and I had the authority of a general."

Disappointed with His Body

"You and your siblings were raised with military structure. Did your dad serve in the army?"

"Yes, when he was younger."

"Was his time in the army successful?"

"Yes, he achieved wide-reaching recognition."

"How far up into the ranks did he climb?"

"He became a captain."

"Did he end his military career because he was leaving to do something else, or had he just reached the end of the line?"

"Something happened to one of his legs, but he had a lot of contacts and used them to become an import and export merchant."

"So, your dad raised you based on his military background?"

"Yes," Jarl says proudly.

"Did you join the army too?"

Jarl falls silent.

"You didn't join the army."

"Something was up with my breathing. It was fragile, so they didn't think it would have been appropriate for me to join the army."

"Taking your upbringing into consideration, how did you feel about not being good enough for the army?"

"I rose above it. It was not because there was an issue with my psyche, intelligence, or mental abilities. It was something physical, and even the best of soldiers can be limited by their physique, just like with my dad and his leg."

"Were you disappointed about not getting into the army?"

"I was disappointed with my body, but my dad pointed me in a different direction where I could still exert influence seeing as I had this natural authority and ability to pass on knowledge."

"Did you find a wife?"

"Yes."

"Where do you meet her?"

"At a private party."

"Were the hosts acquaintances, friends, or people your parents know?"

"They were friends of my parents."

"What was she doing when you met her? Was she educated?"

"She'd been trained as a maid."

"Was she nice?"

"Yes."

"Was she talented?"

"Very…she made delicious food."

"What about you and your wife, did you have kids?"

"Yes, two of them."

"And were you okay with only having two kids even though you're from a family of eight kids?"

"No, and they were both girls."

"Did them both being girls change your relationship with your wife?"

"It was not her fault. The birth of the second proved difficult and was a physical shortcoming for her."

"Was she fine other than that? Were the kids well?"

"Yes."

The Warden

"Did you experience other challenges in the time that followed?"

"I was offered the warden position at the orphanage."

"How old were your own daughters at that time?"

"Teenagers."

"Did you have any thoughts about this position at the orphanage?"

"I thought it was the right step to take next."

"You applied for the job. Did you get it?"

"Of course, and we ended up living in an extension of the orphanage."

"Was it a home for abandoned kids, kids with special needs, or kids who couldn't seem to behave."

"They were older kids who weren't of age and who struggled with discipline."

"Where was it?"

"Here in the south, so we left my hometown."

"So, you had your own house at the orphanage, you were the warden, and you were in charge of everything."

"Yes, just the way I like it."

"What was it like at first, surely there was a lot of tidying up to do?"

"Yes, there were some wrongs to right, and I did that."

"How did you right the wrongs at an orphanage?"

"Through strict discipline, of course."

"Can you give me some examples of strict discipline at the time?"

"You were allowed to discipline the kids physically."

"You were allowed to hit them?"

"You were and you did."

"I get the feeling that you eventually put the place in order, but I also feel like some conflicts arose?"

Jarl falls quiet and didn't answer.

"Did that have anything to do with your own kids? Were you disappointed with their behaviour, or what happened?"

"I'm not interested in talking about it."

"How did you and your wife respond to the conflict?"

"My wife got very mad at me."

"Why?"

"She thought I disciplined my daughter too harshly."

"Was this the older or the younger one?"

"The older one."

"What were the consequences?"

"She ran away from home."

"Did she run away by herself, or was she with someone?"

"I don't want to tell you that."

"My guess is that she left with someone from the orphanage. Am I wrong?"

Jarl stays quiet.

"Were you more disappointed that she defied you, that she left with someone from the orphanage, or that people started talking?"

"That she defied me. She was dragging the family name through the mud."

"Did they go far?"

"I don't know."

"Did you talk to her again, or did something happen to her?"

Jarl is silent as the grave.

"Jarl, did you hurt your daughter mentally or physically when you disciplined her?"

"I did, and rightfully so. She yelled that they were calling me the Dictator, General, Major, and so on. Those were just other words for 'great', but 'the Dictator' had an ugly, condescending feel to it."

"Did you kill her?"

Jarl doesn't answer.

"Maybe you didn't hear my question, so I'll ask again. Did your daughter die because of how you disciplined her?"

"There could easily have been another explanation, maybe she had a weak heart."

"Right, it could just as easily have been something physical."

"It could have."

"So, she didn't actually run away, but suddenly, she was not there anymore. Did people start asking about her, like her mom, her sister, or the boy from the orphanage? Did anyone know that you'd taken her life?"

"My wife knew what had happened."

The Rumours Spread

"What did you do with your daughter's body? Did you bury her, put up a headstone, or…?"

"Of course not."

"You were setting a really good example for your younger daughter…"

Jarl nods decisively.

"Had anyone started asking about her whereabouts?"

"Yes, the rumours were spreading, but I didn't care about rumours. The only thing that matters is whether you can prove it."

"What kind of rumours? That she'd run away, or that she was dead?"

"A mix of both."

"Was your wife your ally under the circumstances, or did your relationship start to crumble?"

"She stopped talking to me that day…She still cooked for me and ironed my shirt, but she didn't talk to me."

"I get the feeling that the years that followed were turbulent. What was the age difference between your two daughters?"

"Two years."

"Your younger daughter grows up. What happens when she reached the age that her older sister was when she died? Did conflicts arise with her?"

Jarl grows quiet.

"What did she do? I sense that a rebellion of sorts was on its way?"

"She told me that she wanted to travel."

"Had she ever asked you about her sister?"

"No."

"Did she see what happened, or did she know?"

"Maybe she heard it happen...She was home that day."

"Do you feel like she was old enough to travel?"

"She was only 14 years old, but she wanted to travel with a Christian school."

"How did you feel about that?"

"It was an option."

"In what way?"

"It tended to be women who went on missions...they were very strict and big on discipline, and that way she wouldn't be tempted by the boys at the orphanage."

"That was perfectly aligned with your beliefs. What about your own upbringing, was religion a part of that?"

"We went to church on Sundays...That's what you did back then, and that's where you met the other people in town."

"What was your decision? Did you think that was a good path for her?"

"She went on the trip."

"Was it with your blessing?"

"Yes, she went to Africa where she was going to help set up a Christian school, and then she'd be going out to find students."

"Did you see her again?"

"No."

"Did you hear from her?"

"Through letters, but they were addressed to her mom."

"So, the two of you didn't communicate?"

"No."

"Did you try to contact her at any point?"

"When my wife wrote back, she used 'we' at my request."

The Attack

"Let's go back home, you must have been in your 50s at this point?"

"Getting up there, yeah."

"How were things between you and your wife? How was your relationship? Did you still have a relationship?"

"She still didn't talk to me."

"That had been going on for a few years by now."

"She only spoke to me when we had guests and only out of politeness."

"How did you feel about living this way? Was it satisfactory for you?"

"It was a big sacrifice to make, but there were always victims along the way."

"Everything has its price. But did you stay at the orphanage for the rest of your working life?"

"Yes, right up until the day I died."

"Was your wife present when you died?"

"No, I was alone."

"How had you been feeling in the leadup to your death? You were around 60, so what happened? Did your asthma get worse?"

"Not exactly...I got attacked by undesirables."

"These undesirables, were they from the orphanage?"

"Maybe."

"What were the consequences? Were you physically injured?"

"There were four men and I must have had a weak heart."

"Did you know any of the men who attacked you? Had you seen them before?"

"I had."

"Where had you seen them before?"

Jarl falls quiet.

"Did one of them happen to look like your older daughter's boyfriend?"

"Happened to look like him...Yes."

"So, it was payback, and you paid with your life?"

"They threw me into a ditch."

"Looking back at your life and what you'd done, do you feel that you deserved that? Did you see it coming, or did it happen out of nowhere? After all, this is a taste of your own medicine."

"My goal had always been to bring out the best in people," Jarl states, somewhat indignantly.

"Yes, but had you ever considered the consequences of your methods? That the price you had to pay, aside from your daughter's life, was your own life? Had you never considered pausing and re-evaluating your approach to bringing out the best in people?"

"I did what I thought was best."

"Right, because you just did what you'd been taught."

"You got recognition and respect for directing the troops with a fair, albeit sometimes hard, hand. Anything else would lead to mutiny."

"You were beaten to death and thrown into a ditch. When did you realise that you were dead?"

"I went back home to my wife, but she didn't talk to me."

"But this time, it's because she couldn't hear you. Did you know that?"

"I figured that out. The police came to our house once someone found my body. They asked her if I had any enemies, and she chuckled, which they found strange, and then she explained that I wasn't a particularly well-liked person."

"How did you react when you heard her say that to the police, and when you saw her breathe a sigh of relief because the Dictator was gone?"

"I thought to myself that I needed to spend time with like-minded people who understood me and looked at life the same way I did."

"Do you ever think that your life might have taken a different trajectory if you had done things differently?"

"No."

"So, you left your home?"

"I didn't have a reason to stay."

"You went out into the world. Did you find like-minded people?"

"Yes, right here."

"Who did you find here?"

"Important business people."

"Were these physical people or were there other ghosts to talk to?"

"What do you mean?"

"Was Torben living here with his family when you came to this house?"

"No, no...I got here much earlier than he did. In the late 60s, I think."

"Who was here at that time, and what did they represent?"

"There was a meeting that I found interesting, so I stayed. I think the place has a certain kind of authority."

"There have been many residents in this house since then."

"Yes, many different people have lived here, but I've always been able to find a family member who had the same notable beliefs as me."

"I know that the place used to be home to a religious cult."

"That's correct."

"Were their beliefs aligned with your own?"

"I was fine with them. It wasn't about who they were or what they were; it was their beliefs that I found interesting. As in, I called the shots here, and that was not up for negotiation. The strength to stand by your beliefs even if you're met with resistance – I respect that."

"How have you been feeling lately, now that there's nobody in the house and Torben and his family have been away for more than a year?"

"I'm kind of bored. There haven't been as many good discussions as there usually were."

"Have you had some time to look back on your life?"

Jarl looks at Torben.

"You're the diametrical opposite of me. You're far too gentle, but I liked your wife. She was strict and had clear beliefs."

"Would she have been a good wife for you?"

"No, you can't have two people calling the shots in a marriage. She would've been too much to handle."

"Even for you?"

"Especially for me. I'm the captain, and I'm in charge."

"You've spent some time by yourself now, Jarl. Have you thought about whether there's anything you regret?"

"I regret not being able to keep my daughters away from the orphanage. Maybe we should've lived in town and commuted to the orphanage. There was no way for those two worlds to coexist. My oldest daughter went to a great school in town, but she hung out with the orphanage kids after school."

"Did you ever think that what did happen could happen? Was it maybe even something you feared?"

"Never! It took me completely by surprise. For generations, we'd been surrounding ourselves with the right people, so it baffles me that my children would fraternise with people of a different class."

Dreaming of the Circus

"From your life story, I can tell that you've done as you were asked and achieved good results based on what you learned at home, but it's had some serious consequences. I sense that you're walking around with grief, and perhaps even sadness, because there was something you couldn't change or influence, and you can't tell anyone about it."

"I'm not sure what that's about. Do you have a guess?"

"I think when you were about seven or eight years old, you found yourself in a situation where you had to shut down your feelings about the freedoms you wanted. You've told us how your life has been but not the feelings you've had about it. I think you used to have dreams back when you dared to dream."

"I honestly don't remember that."

"It's about a close childhood friend. Someone who wasn't like the others."

"The maid in my childhood home had a son who was about my age."

"So, aside from your mom, you had a maid to help out around the house?"

"Yes, there were many duties. She also helped prepare the house for business meetings and the likes."

"Did your parents stay together?"

"Yes, they're together for life."

"What was the name of the maid's son?"

"I don't remember."

"I get the feeling that you had something special. Whenever you were together, you see opportunities, and you dreamed together. What did you dream about?"

"We dreamed of travelling with a circus."

"You liked playing circus, but why specifically circus?"

"It was just a childhood dream. It was fun."

"At some point, someone put an end to your dream. What happened to your friend?"

"Only gypsies and other undesirables travel with the circus."

"Was your good friend a gypsy?"

"No."

"Was he an undesirable?"

"Not in my opinion."

"What happened to him or to you? I get the feeling that your relationship had consequences."

"My dad told me that I couldn't play with him anymore."

"What did your dad say?"

"If you hang around with undesirables, you become an undesirable."

"And you didn't want to be an undesirable?"

"Does anyone?"

"What does the word 'undesirable' mean to you?"

"People without social status. Like homeless people."

"What happened after you'd been told that you couldn't play with him anymore? Did you try to meet up in secret or was it over for good?"

"We tried to talk to each other when nobody was looking."

"How did that go?"

"Not well."

"Did you get caught?"

"Yes, and his mom lost her job because of it."

"So, she lost her job. Did they move?"

"Of course."

"Did you ever see each other again?"

"Of course not…We were from different worlds."

"Did you think of him as you grew older?"

"I haven't thought about him in years."

"I think maybe you've packed away the memory of what happened then, but how do you feel about us talking about it right now?"

"They're fun memories."

"Looking back on your life, are there any memories that come close to the ones you had with the maid's child?"

"Different ones, at least."

"What ties you together isn't so much what's going to happen or what could happen but rather the feeling of freedom."

"Yes, it's the adventure...a new town every day."

"I think what happens is that all these dreams about freedom and adventure are shattered when your dad imposes his expectations on you, and you chose to bottle up your feelings because your dad expected a lot and the adventure was too much to think about. And then you did what your family has always done: create results without thinking about feelings or consequences."

"You didn't get far on feelings alone; you had to use your intellect."

"Because what happens when you depend on your feelings?"

"You make inappropriate decisions."

"Try to tell me about an inappropriate decision you've made back when you dared to feel. I don't believe you've always been the way you are now."

"I was the one who convinced him to come out to play even though we weren't allowed. I didn't think anything would happen."

"But something did happen. He got sent away, and at that age, you had to do as your dad told you."

"Yes, and make sure never to make the same mistake again."

"And you didn't. But it's interesting that history repeats itself with your older daughter. Do you see the connection?"

"Maybe."

"She also played with someone who wasn't appropriate for her."

"I think they did more than play."

"But you told her that she couldn't play with him just like your father told you that you couldn't play with your friend."

"So far, so good."

"When your dad found out that you were playing together, the maid lost her job, and instead of sparing your daughter that experience, you did exactly the same thing your father did. You even took it one step further by disciplining her so harshly, she died as a result."

"I didn't mean for her to die...I just wanted to teach her a lesson."

"There are many ways to do that. Do you see the connection between you and the maid's son and your daughter and the boy from the orphanage? You actually got the option to choose a different path than your father did, an opportunity to change a pattern that hurt you deeply as a child."

"I think there's a difference between playing with an eight-year-old and doing what my daughter was doing with that man."

"As I see it, it's about the way you felt with your friend. You met someone who made you feel free and someone you wanted to go on adventures with. That's what your daughter had with that man."

Jarl is quiet for a while before he answers.

"I didn't think of it that way."

"I'm sure you didn't, but looking back at your life, does that make sense?"

"There's a certain satisfaction to be found in following the rules and seeing your dreams come true." Jarl turns to Torben.

The Gentle Man

"You're not the same kind of man as I am. You're a gentle man, but you're still a man of a certain status. How would you feel if your daughters fraternised with boys of a completely different status?"

"If it's a matter of the heart, it's up to them. I wouldn't take issue with that," Torben answers.

"It wouldn't bother you at all?"

"I recognise your story because I've experienced something similar. My dad had firm beliefs when it came to what I should and shouldn't do. So, I think my dad would frown upon my daughters finding partners who, in his eyes, weren't of the same status as we are."

"Did your father choose your friends for you too?"

"Whenever I brought friends or girlfriends over, my dad always asked, 'What does your father do?'."

"Mine did too. Did your father also turn away your friends if they didn't give him an answer he liked?"

"No, I don't remember him ever doing that, but he did sometimes make me feel bad about my choices. But in other situations, he's shown me that there was a heart beneath that hard exterior of his. One of my friends, who had the lowest social status of them all, was dyslexic and struggled at school. In the beginning, my dad used to ask me what I was doing hanging out with him, but my dad actually ended up taking my friend under his wing, giving him an apprenticeship in his company and actively supporting him through the years. He accepted that there was a person behind the lack of obvious academic qualifications, even though his general outlook was the exact opposite," Torben continues.

"Jarl, do you recognise this feeling of guilt that Torben mentions?" Laurens asks.

"After the maid's son, I've never tried to make friends with people of a different social status. We went to a private school, and that world was miles from the public school. You naturally made friends with the people your family surrounded themselves with and the kids you met in school, so we kept to ourselves. That was the safest option."

"What did you think about Torben's story about the boy who was given an apprenticeship by Torben's dad?"

"My father probably wouldn't have done that."

"It could've been your brother."

Jarl falls silent.

"You're right, it could've been my brother. My father just said that he wasn't right in the head, and we just followed the path he laid out for us. That was unfortunately part of it." Jarl pauses briefly and turns to Torben. "You were luckier than my brother and me. But why haven't you become a hard man like my father? How do you grow up without becoming your father?"

"That's a really good question," Torben answers. "I've been asking myself that question – why have I become the exact opposite of my father? I've always looked up to him, and still, I've chosen a different path. Not in terms of my profession but in terms of his social status."

"You don't usually see sons who look up to their fathers deciding to take such a humanitarian path. What have you done?"

"For the longest time, I made the same decisions as my dad, choosing a sport and an education that he approved of." Torben pauses for a moment and continues. "But then someone came along who made me re-evaluate my decisions and change my priorities, so they were no longer like my father's."

"I've never met a person who could do that," Jarl says.

"When someone speaks to your heart, that disrupts your way of life. It'll stabilise in time, but it takes courage," Laurens says.

"And then you met this one," Jarl looks over at Pernille. "She reminds me of my oldest daughter."

"In that case, I understand why you didn't like me or had a hard time accepting me at the beginning," Pernille says.

"Your life was what it was, but can you see that there are some things you should have taken a closer look at?"

"I'm very fascinated by Torben's story. We had a similar upbringing, but he chose a different path. I can't believe that's possible. I don't think it's easy to decide to grow up into a different person than your father if you have a firm father like we did." Jarl looks at Torben. "I would've liked to have some of what you have, to have the ability to become someone else without it causing an uproar. To enjoy the best of both worlds. It's interesting, and it's been a while since we've had a good meeting in this room."

A Catch-up

"How do you feel, Jarl?" Laurens looks at Jarl.

"I'm good. I can feel that a change is coming."

"What do you gain from being in this house. What makes you stay?"

"Up until today, I've enjoyed seeing other people exert their influence. Observing leaders, seeing how they administer discipline and choose their courses of action. But you've given me something to think about. I used to think in terms of 'either, or', but you've shown me that sometimes there's space for everything," Jarl explains.

"Have you had other ghosts here, or are you all alone?" Torben asks.

"There used to be a homeless man in the stables, but I sent him on his way. But there's a lot of residual unhappiness around the house that probably makes the rooms feel heavy. Now you can walk through the rooms of the house and shake off the house's past. When you do that, you'll move away from the either-or era and towards a more open-minded future."

"Jarl…" Laurens says.

"I can hear them calling my name."

"Someone's come to pick you up, so I think it might be about time. I'd like to thank you for telling us your story about living a life governed by arbitrary rules and figuring out that you have a choice, if you want it."

"Apparently so," Jarl says, his voice lighter.

"In my experience, you can't deal with the problem until you've located it. But someone's here to greet you." Laurens steps aside.

"It's the maid's son. He's grown into a man. He looks good for his age," Jarl says.

"I think a catch-up is due. And maybe a pick-me-up," the maid's son says.

Jarl rises from the chair.

"You'll have to entertain yourselves from now on. Thanks for the chat. It's been a while since I've had such a good conversation."

Jarl and the maid's son leave the room, and they fade as they walk.

"How do you feel about that, Torben?" Laurens asks.

"I'm fine, but what a story! And there are so many crossovers with my own life, but I can see that I'm on the right path given the rules I had as a child. I'm going to keep living my life at my own pace because looking back, I see that I've made a lot of progress," Torben answers.

'Shortly after this conversation, Torben's farm was sold.'

Chapter 9
Alfred's Shock
Stop Being Mad at Yourself

Susanne lives in a house in northern Zealand with her husband and his two kids. They've been living together for almost four years; however, Susanne finds it difficult to unite the two families. She has a daughter from a previous relationship who's now at boarding school. She feels like the task grows more insurmountable by the day, and she's getting tired. Now she's reached out for help because she feels a heavy sadness around the house. A ghost with a tragic background appears and gives us an insight into how harshly and unnecessarily we judge and punish ourselves; a lesson in the importance of learning to forgive ourselves.

"Can I ask who you are?" Laurens asks in the bedroom that doubles as an office. He started here with Pernille and Susanne because this is the room in the house that seems to have the heaviest energy.

"My name is Alfred."

"Why are you here?"

"I'm observing the family."

"Have you been doing that for a long time?"

"Yes, it's been many years."

"Many years? Go on…"

"I don't remember how many, but it's been a while."

"What happened?"

"It's horrible, but I'm not sure I'm ready to talk about it."

"Okay, then let's start somewhere else. Where were you born, and where do you come from?"

"I was born in a town in what's now known as Sweden but was considered part of Denmark back in my day."

"Were there a lot of kids in your family?"

"Three of us had the same mom, but our mom died giving birth to her third child."

"Your mother died. Did the child survive?"

"Yes, that child was me."

"How did that affect the family?"

"My dad remarried soon after. There were a lot of things to take care of with three boys."

"Did your dad and his new wife have any kids?"

"Yes, they had five kids together, so there were eight of us total, but that was completely normal at the time."

"Were your younger siblings girls or boys?"

"Two girls and three boys."

"So, given the norms at the time, having all those boys meant that you had a pretty solid family."

"Yes, we were born to work with our hands. We started working as soon as we were old enough to hold the tools."

"Was this in an agricultural or a farm setting?"

"It was in a farm setting, and there were a few fields to tend to. We worked the land, but harvesting didn't take long with so many kids, so we also helped out on the surrounding farms. We were very popular."

"How were things at school?"

"We had a traditional education which focused on learning to read, write, and do arithmetic...other than that, we just worked."

"What was the age difference between your oldest brother and your youngest brother or sister?"

"My dad had eight kids in just over ten years. He used to say that he hit his mark once a year."

"Did you or your siblings have any problems at school?"

"I didn't have any problems, and as far as my siblings go, I don't remember there being any major issues either."

"Was it a big or a small school?"

"It was the only school in the area."

"How many years of school did you complete at that time?"

"Six. I think I was about 12, maybe 13 years old, when I left school."

"And you were good with your hands?"

"Absolutely," Alfred answers.

"You continued to help out on the farm in the years that followed?"

"Yes."

"About four or five years after you left school, something happened that changed your family?"

"Yes, my father's brother got in an accident and needed help taking care of the animals and working his land. He didn't have a lot of children because he lost his first wife, with whom he didn't have any, and the kids he had with his second wife were still too young to be able to help out."

"How did his first wife die?"

"She got a lung infection and died after a rough winter."

"Did he live far away from you?"

"Yes, he lived up in northern Zealand."

"Did you go alone, or did you bring someone with you?"

"I brought my oldest younger brother. He was two years younger than me."

"It was a long journey, especially seeing as you were not very old…"

"Yes, it was a long journey but also an interesting one, because we haven't been there before."

"Had you ever been to Zealand before?"

"No, this was the first time."

"You were going from Sweden to Denmark. What was it like sailing for the first time?"

"I experienced a bit of nausea, but I thought it was exciting. I couldn't swim."

"In that case, you might have been a little extra nervous…"

"I really was."

"Do you remember where you sailed from?"

"North of Malmö and Copenhagen. It took around three days."

"Did you get picked up at the docks, or did you have to find your way to your uncle's house by yourselves?"

"We got picked up by horse."

The Woman with the Eggs

"What was it like, arriving in north Zealand and meeting your family?"

"It was exciting, and we were happy to help. We'd helped out a lot of people already, but it was the first time we were this far away from home, so we thought that was fun. My uncle was very impressed, but my aunt said that we ate a lot."

"So, life with your aunt and uncle was good?"

"Yes."

"What did you get into when you weren't working?"

"The way I remember it, we worked most of the time, but other than that we went to the market, and in the fall, we went to the harvest ball."

"Aside from the girls, what did you find interesting about the market?"

"Trade and life…when you were out in the fields all day, you spent a lot of time with yourself. At the market, there were horses and oxcarts, and you could buy all sorts of things."

"How about the coming years? Was there any sort of agreement as to how long you'd be staying?"

"We were just supposed to be there over the summer and finish the harvest in the fall but seeing as my uncle kept getting weaker and we liked being there, we agreed to stay indefinitely."

"And you were both happy with that decision."

"Yeah, we both were."

"Did your uncle's condition worsen as time went on?"

"It didn't worsen, but it didn't get better. It was something with his hand."

"Let's go three to four years into the future. Where were you at in life?"

"I met my wife."

"Where did you meet your wife?"

"She sold eggs at the market."

"Was she nice?"

"I thought she was nice."

"How many eggs did you buy before you asked her if she'd like to come out dancing or maybe go for a cup of coffee?"

Alfred laughs.

"Many, especially considering we had our own chickens."

"Did she live nearby?"

"She lived close to our village."

"You finally plucked up the courage to ask her. Was it hard?"

"Isn't it always?"

"Of course, I guess that hasn't changed. Did you live separately, or did you move in together?"

"You didn't move in together until you were married."

"Was it long before you were married?"

"I proposed to her the first time we spoke. She blushed a little and smiled at me. Every time I talked to her after that, I asked her to marry me, and she eventually said yes. Her mom called me the persistent suitor. But they ended up giving her permission to marry me. When she finally said yes, that was a big day."

"Was she older or younger than you?"

"A couple of years younger."

"How long between the day she said yes and the day you got married?"

"Not very long at all. A month or two. I'd been saving up for a while, and I hadn't had anything to spend my money on. My uncle always insisted on giving us some money for helping him out, even though we were coming over to help because he was family...so I saved up the money he paid me, so I could afford a wedding."

"And the wedding, was that a good day?"

"Very much so. It was a joyful day."

"Did any of your family members from the other side of the sound attend?"

"Two of my siblings came. We'd chosen to get married in the middle of the harvest season, so it was hard to find time to get away, but I couldn't wait until next spring, and it was a rough journey to make in the winter."

"Did you move in together once you were married?"

"Yes, her family owned a large property, so we built a house a little further out on their land."

"Did you start building before or after the wedding?"

"Shortly before the wedding because when I asked her father for her hand, he suggested building our house on his property. It was a big place, so there was plenty of space for everyone."

"Was that a good idea?"

"I thought so because family values have always meant a lot to me."

"What about your younger brother? Did he help you build your house?"

"He helped, and the even younger brothers who came to the wedding stayed a little longer to help out as well."

"Did it take you long to build the house?"

"It was hard work because we were still working out in the fields during the day, so we didn't get around to building until we were off for the night. We had a little more time on our hands in the late fall, when the harvest was done, but it was also a lot colder. The house was done come spring."

"What about your younger brother? Did he move in with you or did he stay with your uncle?"

"He stayed with our uncle. It was not too far away."

"So, only you and your wife moved into your house?"

"Yes, it was a wonderful time in our lives."

"Had you been dreaming about this for a while?"

"I'd probably been dreaming about it for longer than my wife because I'd always known she was the one."

The Band of Robbers

"Did you still work for your uncle or father-in-law after you moved in and started a family of your own?"

"I still worked for my uncle and I was happy to do it, but money was tight. My wife's family knew that I was helping my uncle, so they helped us out at first. Not with money but we did start swapping this and that. My wife was a good seamstress, so she made sure we had clothes to wear. We had more than enough in the way of animals and crops from my uncle's farm and my wife's family... Those were good, happy times."

"What about kids?"

"We had a daughter a year and three months after the wedding and a second daughter the year after."

"What was it like being a father and having your own family?"

"It was out of this world. I didn't want a huge family because every time my wife got pregnant, I was scared of losing her."

"Just like you lost your mother?"

"Yes. I didn't want to be the cause of another woman's death."

"So, things were fine, but there were more mouths to feed?"

"Yes, my wife suggested getting some animals and growing our own crops. She encouraged me to split my time between my uncle's farm and our place. His farm is about half an hour away on horseback, so it was nearby, and I was happy to split my time. So, I talked to my uncle and he was understanding. He asked me if I could stick around until he found someone to replace me. I asked around and had my wife's 14-year-old brother in mind. He was happy to help if I taught him the ins and outs of the job."

"Did your wife's younger brother help you or did he help your uncle?"

"He started helping my uncle. I stayed at home and worked for myself."

"How did that work out?"

"At first, my uncle wasn't too happy with the exchange, but my wife's brother got the hang of it quickly. As you can tell, we were a close-knit family, so there were expectations. You were there for each other."

"You'd been there for other people your entire life, and now you had to be there for yourself and your family. Was that difficult for you? Did you feel guilty?"

"No, but I might've had a hard time if my uncle had been a demanding man. Luckily, he was a man who knew how his own injury limited him, so he knew he should be grateful for the time and help he got, and he understood that I needed to go out and live my own life. I stayed in the area, so he had someone to reach out to if things were about to go up in flames."

"Did anything go up in flames over the years?"

"Yes, speaking of flames, one of the houses in the area burned down."

"Did anyone get hurt?"

"No people were hurt, but some of the animals burned in the stables. We helped out even though they were not family. We had a good community."

"So, things were looking up. You were in your mid-20s and you had your life ahead of you, but then something happened?"

"Yeah, I was around 30 years old and my kids were five and four respectively." Alfred pauses. "There'd been a meeting at the market because a band of robbers had been stealing from farms in the neighbouring towns. Story goes there are six to eight men on horseback. We didn't know where they'd come from, only that they targeted the farms on the outskirts. The farms where they could be in and out."

"What did you think when you heard those stories?"

"I thought, 'Why would they come to our town?' We're a peaceful community of honest people who work hard and get on with our work. People like that have no business in our community."

"So, you didn't think there was a possibility that it'd happen to you?"

"We agreed that the farms on the outskirts needed to keep an eye out and start arming themselves."

"Did you do that so you could protect your family and your values?"

"Yes, but I still felt weird about having an external threat in our midst. I mean, we were not the perfect community. We'd had thieves run off with cattle and steal the occasional trinket at the market and we'd seen fights between young men who couldn't agree on who was courting whom, but we'd always managed to resolve our issues and put the guilty parties before the judge. This was different. When you didn't know who the culprit was. The myths and the stories ran amok. That made it even scarier. So, I showed my wife how to use the rifle in case anything happened while I was out of the house."

"What happened?"

"One night, I had to go deal with some things in the stables, and the building was a fair distance from our house. It was almost dark. Then I heard the sound of horses galloping, and I knew exactly what was happening. Suddenly, I couldn't move. My feet refused to move. I was frozen in my place and then I heard my wife screaming. I heard the rifle being fired, followed by more gunshots. There were an awful lot of them, and then the sound of horses galloping away shortly after. When my legs finally let me move again, I sprinted across the field and into the house. I saw my wife lying with the rifle by her side. She'd been shot, as had both of my kids. They were lying behind her. I imagined she told them to hide behind her in an effort to protect them when she started firing at the robbers. There was blood by the door, so she must've hit some of the robbers, and they must've fired back, hitting both my wife and our kids before running away. Maybe the reception surprised them."

"What did you think when you saw their corpses?"

"I don't know. I don't think I was thinking at all."

"That's understandable. You were in shock because the thing you feared most – being the cause of another woman's death – just happened."

Alfred nods quietly.

"Maybe things would have been different if your legs had been working, so maybe you are responsible for another woman's death. 'Maybe'."

"It was not just another woman's death. It was my beloved wife and my two young daughters. In that moment, I felt like I had nothing left. I didn't know where they were going, but I wanted to go with them."

"What you'd always wanted, and what kept you going, was gone."

"I heard things going on outside. Screaming and noise. I think it was her family rushing to our help, but I can't imagine living in the house without them. I wanted to be with them, so I took the rifle, put in new cartridges, and shot myself."

"That's a violent way to go, but you died, and your body fell to the ground. Then what did you do?"

"I watched the scene from above. My wife's family came in, and they sprinted straight to our bodies. They shook the two small girls, but they didn't move…They screamed and shouted and didn't understand what'd happened."

"What did you do once the situation had calmed down? Did you stay in the house, or did you start looking for your wife and kids?"

"It's all a blur. I left the house after our funerals. Everyone in the area was talking about it, and they guessed right: I was in the stables, and my wife tried to defend herself until I reached them, and when I reached them, I killed myself. Nobody blames me…except myself. They all think I tried to

170

reach them. I'm the only one who knows that my legs refused to move, and I can't bear to think that I'm leaving such a rosy legacy because I don't deserve it. If a man offs himself because he can't live without his wife, he's a hero or something special. I'm neither a hero nor something special."

"Your dad and uncle both kept living even though they lost their wives. Of course, they didn't lose their kids, but they did find love again."

"Yes, but they lost their wives to something that was beyond their control."

"That's true. It wasn't their fault."

"So, I left the region. I couldn't find my wife; I couldn't find my kids, and I couldn't stay in town, bearing witness to all the pain my family suffered in the aftermath of losing us all. I walked away, and I kept walking until I reached the sea."

"Did you meet anyone that you tried to reach out to on your way, or did anyone try to talk to you?" Laurens asks.

"Someone tried to talk to me. He told me not to be so hard on myself. I asked him to leave me alone because I wanted to be hard on myself."

The Time by the Sea

"What did you do when you reached the sea?"

"Well, I found some sort of cave in the dunes. I sat down and looked out at the sea. I sat there for many years, watching life on the beach."

"What were you watching for? Were you expecting something or someone to show up and change what had happened?"

"We used to punish people who had done horrible things by banishing them. We made them leave town, leave their friends, family, and acquaintances...I'd always been a family man, and I'd always enjoyed the company of other people, and I didn't feel like I deserved the company anymore. If the people around town had known the truth, I'm sure they would've banished me. I would've been an outcast. So, I was trying to find a fitting punishment. I isolated myself because isolation is the worst punishment I could think of."

"You force yourself into exile. You didn't talk to anyone for all those years?"

"I didn't talk to other people, and I rejected the ones who tried to talk to me. I did that until I felt like I'd done my time."

"But one day you just got up and started walking. Why did you do that?"

"I don't know. Something about that day was just different."

"Was it the weather, or did you feel like you'd done your time?"

"My legs wanted to walk, so I headed down a narrow path."

"Were you walking with someone?"

"No, it was just me. That day, I spotted the house we're in today."

"Does the house remind you of your own, or what pulled you in?"

"I'm not sure, but something about it seemed familiar. It's like it spoke to me. Appealed to me. I wanted to go inside."

"What happened when you entered the house?"

"There is this family living there."

"What is interesting about this family?"

"It is a father and his two kids with the father's new wife. She's the one who takes care of the kids."

"Do you see any parallels with your own upbringing?"

"I think so…She cares very much about the kids even though they aren't hers. That speaks to me, so maybe it's that, but I can't say."

"You decided to stick around. Can you put yourself in the husband's shoes? His first wife isn't dead, they just didn't agree on how to live their lives."

"I don't know if I can put myself in the husband's shoes. I try to talk to the kids, but they're scared of me, and I realise the new wife in the house can sense a presence. If I express anger, she reacts to it."

"So, you try to reach out to the family with love, grief, happiness, compassion, and frustration – is that right?"

"I don't know. I guess the anger had just become my trusty sidekick over the years, so I suppose that's what I expressed the most."

"So, we're talking about your anger towards yourself. Your self-hatred. From your story, it sounds like you aren't mad at the world or other people, just at yourself. I think you see the same self-directed anger in Susanne, and that that's what causes a reaction."

The Angry Man

"But you've stuck around for a while, observing the family and their lives?"

"I'm the angry man in the house, but I just don't want to move on. I settle for watching other people's families. Rather that, than observing my own family because I'm very close with them, and I don't feel like I deserve to see them."

"So, your truth is that the closest you come to having a family is to observe other people's."

"I had a family, but I lost it, so I don't deserve a new one. I need to stop bringing bad luck into the lives of the people I love."

"Aside from what happened to your family on the farm when the robbers attacked, have you brought bad luck on anyone else?"

"Yes, my mom died because of me."

"Has anyone ever blamed you or told you that her death was your fault?"

"Not that I remember, but I saw the grief on my father's face."

"You were an infant, so do you remember the first time you saw the grief?"

"Maybe I didn't see it. Whenever he was in a melancholy mood, I wondered if it was because he'd lost his wife, but he loved his new wife very much…She was a caring woman who took good care of all of us. She might as well have been our real mother."

"But you've been carrying that guilt on your shoulders all your life."

"Yes."

"Do you direct all guilt at yourself?"

"I guess that's what I do, but you've come to talk to me today, and I feel lighter now that I've shared my story. It's been difficult to talk about it because who wants to talk about a life of failure? It's easier to tell a story if you're the hero and not the villain. I often think about the implications of this no man's land. Where are my family members who died before me? Where are my kids and my wife? My mom and my other relatives? At the same time, I don't really want to know the truth because what if the truth is that they're hiding in the next house over, trying to avoid me?"

"Your childhood and your life have been characterised by this guilt that you didn't realise you were carrying around. Whenever you saw or sensed grief in the people around you, that brought your guilt to the surface."

"Yes. I thought I had a happy life. I had a wonderful family, and the people on my wife's side of the family were good people too."

"So, the only person who blames you and continuously feeds this guilt is you, and when you have the chance to change that, you don't get around to it."

"No, it's not that I don't get around to it. I can't do it. If I'd tried to reach them and not made it in time, it might have been a different story, but I just stood there, frozen in place."

"Did you stand still or did you hide?"

"I was standing by the door. My legs wouldn't move, but I guess you could say I was hiding because I didn't even shout out and come to their rescue. I might not have been able to move my legs, but I could've shouted out, but it was like everything inside me came to a screeching halt."

"I think this is about knowing that you did everything you could in the situation. If you know that, you feel lighter than if you feel like you could've done more. If you did everything in your power to help, you have to find a way to forgive yourself because guilt and shame are harmful emotions."

"You're right, and you can bear that burden for not just many but 'too' many years, and still, it benefits no one."

"How do you feel now?"

"A lot lighter than I did before, but I miss my family."

"Someone's here to see you. They'd like to say hello."
Laurens steps aside.

Alfred's two daughters run over to Alfred, and he falls
onto his knees to hug them. The tears flow freely. After a
while, he looks over to where they came from and sees his
wife, who has come to pick him up. Alfred lowers his gaze in
shame as his wife walks towards him. She hugs and kisses
him.

"There's nothing to feel guilty about. Everything is fine.
Don't you remember our deal that you would spend this life
trying to overcome your guilt?" she says with a smile.

"Now that you mention it, I do remember that. So, you
don't hate or despise me?"

"Of course not." Alfred's wife smiles.

"I completely forgot about our deal. But where are the
others? Where have you been all this time?"

"They're waiting for you," Alfred's wife says and
continues. "We left straight away back in the day because we
weren't weighed down by shame or guilt or anything like that.
But it's time for you to come with us. There are a lot of people
waiting impatiently to see you, and we have a lot to talk
about."

Alfred looks over at Laurens.

"Go ahead. Thank you for visiting Susanne. I think your
story about your life might have given her some things to
think about," Laurens answers.

Alfred takes his wife and kids by the hand and leaves the
room. As they walk, they fade slowly from view until they
disappear completely.

Laurens looks at Susanne and asks, "How do you feel?"

"I feel like maybe my self-directed anger and the way I criticise myself and feel like I can never be good enough for other people and myself should be more about just being good enough for myself. I'm doing enough – I have to find a way to move past my feelings of not being enough," Susanne answers.

Chapter 10
The Lady of the Manor
Take an Honest Look
at Your Surroundings

Gitte and Henrik live in a house in southern Funen. They've been doing renovations on the house for some time but the project is dragging out. The materials don't show up on time, and when they finally arrive, their measurements are all wrong. It's one unexpected inconvenience after the other. Gitte is tired of it, and for a while, she's been wondering if something or someone was trying to stand in their way, or if there might be some other reason they were struggling to finish up the works. They've even considered selling the house but agreed to try to cleanse it first. That's the reason Pernille and Laurens have come to visit, and before long, they meet the lady of the manor who has an important message for Gitte.

The kitchen has been one of the hardest rooms to finish in Gitte and Henrik's house. The room is still a mess, and when Pernille and Laurens come to visit, they immediately notice a heavy energy.

"Who are you?" Laurens asks.

Silence.

"Who are you?" Laurens repeats. "And why are you here?"

"I'm Marta," a voice says.

"Hello, Marta. Why are you here?"

"I'm the lady of the manor," Marta answers.

"Which manor are you talking about?"

"One not too far from here."

"What brings you here?"

"I like being here. It seems familiar."

"Interesting, but won't you tell me a little about where you're from? Do you remember where you grew up?"

"Right here in southern Funen."

"Did you grow up far from here?"

"No, only 10 or 20 miles from here."

"In a town or in the countryside?"

"I suppose everything was the countryside back then compared to these days, but it was in the middle of nowhere."

"What sort of time are we in? The 1800s?"

"1820."

"Did you grow up with your mom and dad?"

"Yes, with my mom, dad, and four siblings."

"Age-wise, what was your relationship with your siblings?"

"I had a brother who was a year older, then there was me, and then there was about a year and a half between each sibling after me."

"What did your dad do?"

"He was a shoemaker."

"Did he have his own store, or did he work for someone else?"

"He worked for his dad in his store, and his plan was to take over the family business when our grandfather couldn't work anymore."

"Was your brother meant to do the same?"

"If he wanted to, I'm sure that was an option."

"What about your mom? Did she stay at home?"

"She did, but before she met my dad, she was a maid. He had been providing for her ever since they met. We owned a small piece of land where we grew our own potatoes and vegetables. We didn't sell any of it."

"So, you were self-sufficient and lived off the land."

"Almost, depending on the harvest."

"Was it normal to exchange things with the neighbouring farms?"

"Yes, but our home wasn't a farm. It was more of a house with a garden that we converted into a vegetable patch. We didn't have any animals."

"How were the years before you started school?"

"Fine."

"And all your siblings were still around by the time you started school?"

"Yes, everyone was happy and in good health."

"You started school. How did you feel about that?"

"It was exciting. I'd always been an imaginative child who daydreamed and thought a lot, and I was very fascinated by the stories they told us. There were poems and songs, and then there was all the romance. I often dreamed of being a princess, I guess. We learned all about the royal family, and they told us about princes and princesses, emperors and people who lived grand lives. I thought that was terribly exciting. We didn't struggle by any means, but we didn't live extravagant lives either. We had food to eat and clothes to wear, and we all had our good health, but we lived a mediocre life."

"Unlike the princesses living in their castles, your life was more or less the same every day?"

"I received a wonderful gift each year on my birthday. In other families, you received practical gifts. Clothes, shoes, and other things you needed, but I didn't need new shoes, and my mom was an excellent seamstress, so for my birthday, I would always get something special that didn't have much use. I just thought it was beautiful."

"What kind of thing would you get?"

"One year, I received a brooch that I polished and polished until it gleamed. Another year, it was an embroidered scarf with such wonderful embroidery, it almost looked fragile. I took infinitely good care of each and every one of my gifts, and they meant a lot to me."

"I suppose we could call you a daydreamer?"

"Whenever I used to help my mom out in the kitchen, she'd tease me and tell me to get my head out of the clouds before the food started burning."

Laurens smiles and asks, "And things were good throughout your schooling?"

"Absolutely," Marta answered.

"Were there any subjects that you were particularly good at?"

"Danish was my strongest subject. I was really good at writing poems, but school was easy for me, and I liked learning."

"So, school was a good place for you?"

"I thrived."

"What about your siblings?"

"If I remember correctly, they also did all right. My brother was better with his hands. I guess that's usually the case with boys. He didn't like poetry much. My youngest sister was like me, she daydreamed about princes and princesses. The other two were a little more pragmatic, and they were strong-willed."

The Gateway to the Upper Middle Class

"You finished school and had a life ahead of you. Were you going out to work, or were you staying at home? What sorts of things were on your mind?"

"I wanted to go out and work and keep learning, so I could become a valued maid or housekeeper and one of the rich families would hire me. I'd always wanted to see what their homes looked like and how they lived."

"And one of the ways to do that was to work for them?"

"Yes, the social classes were very clearly divided back then. The people in the upper middle class didn't mingle with the regular folks or the people you might call the working class. You went to the same stores, sure, but you mingled with your own. But as a housekeeper, a maid, or a cook, you had access to their life. Of course, you were only an observer but still. That was the most luxurious thing I could think about back then."

"So, you set out to find work. Where did you begin?"

"I started with my schoolteacher. She'd always praised me for being hard-working, thorough, and well-behaved, so she asked me if I might be interested in helping her."

"What did you say to that?"

"I accepted, of course."

"How old were you at this point?"

"About 15. I'd be watching her children."

"Was she single?"

"No, she was not single; she was married to a banker, but the men didn't watch the children. They didn't have all that much money, but it was important for them to be able to say that they had a maid. They had a son who was just shy of two years old, and she was due to have what would prove to be a daughter soon, and I was tasked with taking care of the two of them. She'd taken 14 days off."

"So, you were responsible for a two-year-old and a newborn baby?"

"Yes, I'd prepared as best I could. I mean, I hadn't been around newborns since my sisters were born, and I was young back then, but I still think I managed just fine."

"Did you move away from home while you worked for your old teacher, or did you stay?"

"I stayed because it was not too far away. I could walk there in half an hour."

"Were your mom and dad happy that you found work so quickly?"

"Of course, and they weren't going to be deprived of my help at home because I was still around at night…"

The Offer from the Manor

"How long did you work for your teacher?"

"Just under two years."

"Then what happened?"

"I received an offer to work at the manor as a maid. Someone from my school recommended me when they announced that they needed a new maid. Of course, I was sad to leave my teacher with whom I'd developed a close relationship, but I felt ready to move away from home, and this way, I'd get to live at the manor. It felt like the home of a prince and a princess."

"You must have been around 17 at this point?"

"Yes."

"I understand your decision to take the leap. You'd been given an opportunity to realise the dream that you'd had since you were a child."

"It was the most gorgeous, renowned manor in the region, so I accepted the offer immediately."

"So, you moved to the manor?"

"Yes."

"How many servants worked there?"

"There were five of us. Two in the kitchen and then another three."

"Where did you fit in?"

"The kitchen was manned by an elderly, highly experienced woman who had a young maid to help her. Then there was a nurse who exclusively tended to the wife, who was ill. I and the other maid took care of all the other duties and dealt with the general housekeeping."

"What was wrong with the wife?"

"She was very pale, her skin looked like porcelain. She stayed inside at all times, and if she walked more than a short distance, she gasped for air."

"What did the nurse do to help her back to health?"

"She was given herbs and warm wraps over her lungs. She didn't deal well with the heat or the cold. She was very beautiful."

"How old was she when you arrived at the manor?"

"I think she was in her early 30s."

"Do you know if she'd been sick for a long time?"

"She'd always been fragile, but it had gotten worse over the years, and her condition continued to deteriorate while I worked there. I only saw her outside the grand room the first year. It more or less served as her home."

"Was the master of the house older or younger than her?"

"He was five years older."

"Did they have any kids?"

"They had two. One was a girl who had the same illness as her mother, and she died of a lung infection in the middle of a particularly harsh winter when she was 12 years old. The other was a boy. He attended a school in Germany where they had family. He was training to be something or other. I'm not quite sure what. And after the second birth, she was in too delicate a condition to have more children."

"You didn't get the chance to meet the girl, but did you meet the boy? Did he ever come home?"

"He came home for the summer. He looked just like his father, and he was about my age. Maybe a year older."

"Was it an exciting time, working at the manor?"

"I think so. There were lots of dinners. The first time I was asked to help with the serving, I almost dropped a plate into the lap of a very fancy woman because I was looking at her gorgeous brooch. It was gleaming like you wouldn't believe. But before long, I started receiving praise for being hardworking and thorough, especially from the master."

"How was that expressed? Did you get a raise?"

"One time, he was sitting around the dining table with some lavish guests. They look at the silverware, and he says, 'Would you look at that shine! That's a good job. It must've been Marta.'"

"Were you unaccustomed to praise?"

"No, but I hadn't been praised by fancy people before. I'd been told that they can be particularly, shall I say, toxic? But he was always warm and hearty."

"Did you enjoy your time at the manor?"

"Most definitely. I daydreamed about weddings and grand parties."

"Did you dream about the master, his son, or someone else, or what are these wedding dreams about?"

"I dreamed about the master," Marta answers with slight embarrassment.

"You thought the master would be a good match, but what made him more suitable than his son who was your own age?"

"The son was a spoiled boy who just wanted to show how much better he was. He always turned his nose up and felt like he was above us servants."

"So, he was one of the toxic ones?"

"He was one of the arrogant ones. He was polite, but in a cold and distant way. And he was just a boy. He wasn't a man yet."

"But the master was?"

"I thought so."

In Love with the Master

"Time passes. You've been there for about three years. Then what happened?"

"He touched me for the first time. It might sound innocent given this time and age, but he put his hand on the small of my back when he talked to me. I found that to be very intimate."

"How did you feel? What did you think?"

"I felt the heat from his hand where he touched me for a long, long time after he'd moved it. I wrote many poems about it."

"20 years old and in love?"

"Yes."

"Was this your first big love?"

"Yes."

"So, you were 20 years old. How were your siblings?"

"They were fine, no drama to report. Whenever I went home to visit my family, I told them all about what I'd seen and heard. They all thought it was very exciting that I was working at such a fancy place. We sat around and talked about dresses for hours. I mean, my dad didn't want to hear about it, but my youngest sister always got the biggest smile on her face when I told her stories from the manor. It was like disappearing into a different world. We didn't have television back then, so our window to the world was limited."

"Was it nice to visit? Did you have a good relationship with your family?"

"Absolutely."

The Poetry Bubbles Over

"I assume your feelings deepened. How were things in the time that followed?"

"Shortly after the master touched the small of my back, we started to exchange more and more looks. I was very confused but also captivated. It was important that you didn't do anything inappropriate. One wrong word or interpretation from the other servants could end up getting you fired, so I didn't dare take any form of initiative. That wasn't something you did back then. Whenever we were alone, and I was fixing something in his workroom while he worked, I could see him observing me. One day, he told me that he wishes his situation was different."

"Did you ask him what he meant by 'his situation'?"

"Yes, I asked, 'What do you mean by your situation?'. He replied that if it wasn't for the promises he'd made to his wife, he would've liked to have me in his life in a different way."

"What were your thoughts on that response?"

"My heart fluttered with joy."

"Did you think about the fact that he had a wife, or did you feel sorry for him?"

"I was in love. I was mostly thinking that it felt like I was caught up in all this drama and that love has to survive impossible tests before it finally conquers."

"The poetry bubbles over."

"It does."

"Did anything happen beyond you exchanging words in his room?"

"Things happen quickly after that, and within the next six months, it had developed into a genuine affair."

"How old were you at this point, 21, 22 years old?"

"Still only 20."

"Were these secret dates? Did they take place at the manor or in the master and his wife's home?"

"Both, whenever the opportunity presented itself. It was a large area, so he would come up with tasks for me to do late at night. His wife grew weaker as time went on, so he often picked me up and told me that my help was needed in the workroom."

"So, you were free to play, if you will. But what about the other servants? Did any of them start asking questions?"

"Not really, but sort of. The elderly cook once told me that she'd noticed I had a tendency to blush when the master entered the room. 'Don't you go getting any good ideas', she said. 'You are and will always be a servant'."

"In other words, someone had figured out what was happening?"

"Yes, my parents had too. They felt I was at that age where I should start looking around for a husband, and they'd noticed that I didn't pay any attention to the young men and the way they looked at me. On more than one occasion, my mom had to point out that someone had asked for me or looked my way because I didn't notice myself."

"Did you ever tell anyone about your feelings?"

"Not at first, but later on, I confided in my youngest sister."

"How much later?"

"I think it had been about a year, and just like me, she thought it was amazing, and she was sure that he'd choose me. That I just needed to stick it out until his wife passed away. Then I'd have my fairy-tale ending."

"The fairy tale was within reach. You were just waiting for his wife to die, so you could take your place in the inner circle?"

"Yes, because he wanted me. He told me that often, but unfortunately, the circumstances dictated that we must be discreet. He said that he'd found love for the first time in his life. He described his marriage as loyalty and sensibility."

"But then things changed. Go on…"

"I don't know if they changed that much…"

"I'm thinking it got harder and harder to keep your hands off each other."

"When we'd been together for around two years, his wife suddenly took a turn for the worst. The doctor called one night, and we were told that she was dangling between life and death, so we were all walking on eggshells."

Pregnant and Grieving

"Did you take care of his wife, or were you in contact with her at any point?"

"No, I didn't look after her. A nurse and another maid were responsible for helping her. I'd seen her a few times, but I didn't see her around the house much. The 14 days that followed were the longest days of my life because we were all worried, but I was also feeling a sense of shame because I was secretly hoping she would die. Not because she was a bad person but because she was standing in the way of my dream and my true love. And then I discovered that I was pregnant and was over the moon."

"You got pregnant during those 14 days?"

"I realised that I was pregnant, so I must have been about a month along. I thought to myself that this was perfect timing. I felt ready to take my place in the limelight."

"With a child that'll make your bond even stronger than it already was."

"That might be able to help him through the grief."

"But then what happens?"

"The wife continued to cling to life, and I was not sure if I should say something to him about me being pregnant, I mean. I chose to tell him, but he got a strange expression on his face. I interpret it as part of his internal conflict between being respectful of his dying wife and the opportunity to give into his feelings and be with me. Just under three weeks passed, and then she died."

"Did that come as a relief to you?"

"I had very mixed feelings. I was confused, because I was still young and cared about what was appropriate and what wasn't. What's an appropriate period of time to grieve, and when could we declare our love for each other?"

"So, you were planning?"

"I was not planning anything. I didn't really have a say in the matter, but I tried to put the pieces together. When could I expect that something would happen? It's not like I could go out and tell the world about us – he needed to take the lead. What was appropriate? What were the unwritten rules? All that. It was a difficult time with a lot of practical things to deal with like the funeral and cleaning up…going through his dead wife's private property."

"Did anyone notice that you were pregnant?"

"Not yet, but I was only a month and a half along. The next couple of months were very chaotic. He travelled a lot, and he was often gone for 3–4 days at a time. He was visiting her family, which was the family in Germany. He brought some of her personal items to her mother. His son came home to spend some time with his father, so I had to take a backseat, but when nobody was around, I tried to push him. He said that it was too soon in terms of the family's expectations, but that one day, I would, of course, become the lady of the manor. I longed for the day, but I stuck it out because the dream was almost within reach…"

"It must have been hard to live like that. I imagine you lived in a small room, biding your time until you moved two floors up and took your place in the inner circle."

"I had dreamed of sitting at the end of the table many times. Dreamed of having someone serve my food while the master and I looked at each other lovingly."

"I suppose you reached a point where you grew tired of waiting and thought that it was high time something happened. That you could really use a hint as to where this was all going?"

"Yes, and I started showing. He told me that he'd recognise the child as his own, but not right now. Things were still difficult, and it was still too soon. So, I had to lie and say that the child was someone else's."

"Did you tell that story to everyone, or did you tell anyone the truth?"

"Initially, I told that story to everyone, but my parents were sceptical, to say the least. They wanted to meet the man in my life."

"So, they didn't believe you?"

"My dad asked me if the master had taken advantage of me. 'Of course not', I respond furiously. In my opinion, he hadn't. My dad kept asking. He almost marched up to the manor to have a word with the master. My mom told me to do the right thing and marry the young man I had made up. I think she knew the truth, but she was hoping there was actually a young man in the picture."

The Maid's Love Affair

"Mothers can sense a lot about their daughters. What happened next?"

"Well, I got bigger and bigger, and I kept working at the manor. One day, I heard the master tell one of his guests that he was taking good care of me because I'd fallen from grace, and I noticed that he was being praised for taking in a girl in trouble. As time went on, I became worried and started having doubts. But there was a power imbalance, and I was not really in a position to set him an ultimatum. I was very frustrated about not being able to do anything. One day, all the servants were gathered in the kitchen, and the maid who helped me take care of the house told me that she'd met the man of her dreams and that we'd all be surprised when she introduced us to him. The others pushed her to give them a hint, and she nodded, suggesting that it was the man out there. The master. Then the elderly cook giggled and said, 'Oh wow, you're sleeping with the master?' My world shattered into a million pieces, and I asked her how long that had been going on, all the while trying to hide the fact that I was about to throw up. The world was spinning. She got a big smile on her face and said that it had been going on for a while, but that they haven't been able to declare their love for each other yet because of his wife's illness and then her death. A lot of the words she used were the same ones he'd said to me, and when she proudly told us that she'd definitely be the next lady of the manor, I fainted. I fell off the chair, and when I woke up, they were all standing over me. I started to cry and sobbed that my dream had been crushed."

"How far along were you? When were you due to give birth?"

"In about five weeks' time."

"Now that the other girl had told her story, did anyone happen to question your pregnancy as you lied there, sobbing on the floor?"

"They looked at each other with confusion, but nobody questioned anything just then. The elderly cook told the young girl who'd been seeing the master to take over my responsibilities for the day because I was incapacitated by my pregnancy, and the young girl didn't question it further. The cook helped me to bed. She didn't ask me directly, and she was very compassionate. She shook her head and said, 'Oh, darling little girl, what have you gotten yourself into?' and I sobbed as she stroked my hair. I stayed in bed for five days, and he didn't come to see me once during that time."

"Did the master not ask the others about you?"

"I don't know. I told myself that he did, but I didn't know. But I did get permission to go home to my parents where my mom and a midwife from town would help out when the baby came. I was told that the master had said I didn't need to worry about my wages while I was on leave."

"What did your mom and dad say when you came home? You hadn't introduced them to the young man yet."

"My dad didn't say much, my mom kept sending him away. She was very worried, and she wanted to sit me down

194

and talk, but every time I saw the tense look on her face, I broke down into tears. I spent most of my time crying, and her face finally softened."

"Did you tell her your secret?"

Marta nods.

"She told me that my naïve dreams had robbed me of my senses and led me astray and that I'd always been such a hopeless romantic."

"How did she react? Was she mad?"

"She was disappointed, but most of all, she was worried. I clung to the belief that everything would be fine, that he'd come around and think of the life we'd build together when he saw the child. My mom said that we were from separate worlds, and that it was easy for him to just leave me out in the cold, and that there was nothing I could do to prove that he was the father. And she was right. But once I'd given birth to a gorgeous, healthy girl who I decided to call Ella, after the manor, I brought her back to the manor."

The Envelope Filled with Money

"How long after giving birth did you go back?"

"A week later…my mom told me to go and sort out this mess. That I needed to figure out what happened next, no matter what it was. The master looked surprised when I brought the child up to the manor."

"Did you go straight to him, or did you say hi to the others in the kitchen?"

"I walked through the kitchen to say hi to everyone."

"What did they say?"

"They said congratulations and told me that she looked like me. I was hoping they would say that she looked like the master because then he wouldn't have been able to run away from his responsibilities, but the atmosphere in the room was tense because we all knew how hard it is to have a child outside marriage and without a father in the picture. Nobody wanted to ask the hard question. I told them that I needed to go speak to the master to find out if I could keep working at the manor, and they understood that, so I went up to his workroom. I knocked on the door and walked inside with Ella in my arms."

"Did he know that you were coming, or did you just show up?"

"He knew I was coming. Maybe not then and there, but he knew we needed to find a solution because I was still working for him. He stood up when he saw me. There was a strange look in his eyes. He tried to smile, and I say, 'Well, here we are.' He looked uncomfortable and said, 'Let's figure out the best way forward.' I asked him to elaborate. He looked more and more uncomfortable until he finally cracked with a resigned gesture. 'Marta, surely you didn't think that this could ever be more. We're from separate worlds', and I ask 'What about our love? What about everything you promised me?' I can see that he's working up a sweat. He stutters as he says, 'Well, a man says a lot of things when he's in the throes of lust'. I tell him, 'I hear you've been saying those things to other people too.' Then he got mad, and he stood up and said, 'I've been incredibly kind to you. Not everyone would take such good care of a servant who has fallen from grace.' I practically shouted, 'I think you're forgetting that you're the one who did this to me,' and my entire body was shaking. Ella started to scream, so I had to calm her down. He told me that he can never recognise Ella as his own daughter. He was a grieving man who had a moment of weakness, but that was just being human."

"So, he told you exactly what you feared he would?"

"You could say that. He was like a different person. Slippery as an eel. Then he asked me where I wanted to go from here. I answered that I didn't know, and I asked, 'What can I do?' He told me that because I'm a valued and loyal employee, he'd like to help me out financially but that, because of my unfortunate situation, I can't stay at the manor and keep working for him."

"What did he mean when he says he'll help you out financially?"

"He wanted to give me an envelope filled with money to help me start over, and I accepted the offer."

"Was it a lot of money?"

"Three months' wages."

"Was that a lot of money at the time?"

"Of course. I mean, it's three months' wages just like it'd be today."

"You took the money. Then what did you do?"

"Then he asked me to leave. Ella was still screaming, and he told me to take good care of my child but that he had some important work to do and that I was disturbing him."

"Did you leave the manor?"

"Yes, I left the manor."

"Did you talk to the others before you left?"

"No, I left out the front door."

"Where did you go?"

"I stood tall and walked down the street."

The Room

"I imagine your world came tumbling down. It had to hurt that you were right in all your doubts. Did you go home, or what did you do?"

Marta pauses for a long time.

"Did you go home to your mom and dad?"

"No," Marta pauses again. "I rented a room close to the manor."

"Why did you rent a room?"

"I wanted to be close to him. I wanted to see what he was up to. I rented the room from an elderly couple, and I had enough to get by for three months."

"Did anyone else know that you'd rented the room, or was it just you?"

Once again, Marta pauses.

"Did you tell anyone that you'd rented the room?"

Marta doesn't say anything for a while, but then she continues, "I told my parents that I'd be staying at the manor until my situation was resolved, so I was the only one who knew about the room."

"Did anyone ask for you?"

"They thought I was at the manor because where else would I be if I was not at home with them?"

"You rented this room in town for three months. After that, something had to change. What did you do?"

Another long pause before Marta answers.

"I kept a close eye on the manor and the master, whenever he was in the area or out in town. I couldn't just visit the manor, so I kept an eye out..."

"Do you see the master at all during the three months you rent the room?"

Marta didn't answer.

"It was like you existed in a state of shock after leaving the manor. In a world of grief, betrayal, and resignation. I get the feeling you couldn't think rationally."

Another long silence before Marta starts talking again.

"My hopes and dreams had been shattered, and now nobody wanted me because I had a child with someone else."

"What did you do about Ella? Did she stay in the room with you the three months you were there?"

Long pause.

"Yes."

"What happened between you and the master?"

Another silence.

"Did you see him with the woman from the kitchen, or did you see him with any other woman?"

"With another woman."

"So, the woman from the kitchen wasn't in the picture anymore. It was a third woman."

"You would never be seen in public with someone of our class."

"So, when you saw the master with a woman, was she someone from his own class, or did you spot him having a romp in the hay with one of the employees?"

"It was not a romp in the hay. They were strolling down the street together, so she was from his own class. They were walking side by side, and he put his hand on the small of her back when he talked to her. Very discreetly and without being inappropriate."

"How did it make you feel to see him do that to her, knowing that he used to do it to you?"

"It made me mad because it was exactly what he used to do to me."

"What did you do? Did you follow them?"

Marta fell silent and refused to respond.

"Did you think that if you couldn't have him then no one could?"

Marta hesitates for a long time before answering.

"I thought she deserved to know who he was. She had the same expression on her eyes that I did, and I knew she was bourgeois, but I still think she should know what his game was."

"Do you get around to telling her?"

Marta didn't answer.

"Did it become a situation where you lost control and shouted in anger?"

"I didn't mean for it to come out like that, but I had a complete meltdown and lost my temper."

"How did she respond to your breakdown? Did it scare her, did she ask about your situation, or how did she take it?"

Marta pauses.

"It's all a blur, but the way I remember it, it startled her."

"Was she startled by the way you said it or by the whole thing about him having a child with you?"

"She was scared that I'd hurt her."

"Did you?"

"No, but it all fell into place for me, and I don't remember it all too clearly, but I didn't hurt her," Marta says and pauses before continuing. "So, I went home and got Ella. I brought her up to the manor in the hopes that he'd take care of her, so maybe she would get to experience the fairy tale…"

"But that's not what happened. Did you kill the master?"

Long pause.

"No."

"Everything around you was chaos. Did you hurt Ella?"

Another long pause.

"No, but it was all a blur."

The Barn and the Baby

"I get the feeling your life came to an end at the manor. Did you take your own life, or did you get hurt?"

Marta stays silent for a while.

"I walked up to his workroom and put Ella down...This was very difficult for me..." Marta pauses for a long time before she continues. "Then I went out into the barn and hung myself." Long pause. "I wanted to force him to take care of Ella, and I thought maybe he'd take her if I weren't there anymore, and then my daughter would grow up with the bourgeois."

"When did you realise that you were dead?"

"When I saw myself hanging there."

"You were dead, and now you could walk around the manor. Did you do that?"

"Yes."

"Do they find you in the barn?"

"Yes, they found me, and the rumours started circulating immediately, and it didn't take long for people to guess that he might be Ella's father. My parents were devastated, and they asked for Ella."

"What did you do? Did you stay at the manor?"

"Yes, because now I could go anywhere."

"What was that like for you?"

"I was very mad and bitter. He should've taken my daughter now that I'd sacrificed myself to give her a chance at a better life, but he gave Ella to my parents as if that were the only plausible option."

"He still didn't recognise her as his own?"

"Not even close."

"So, you got mad again?"

"Yes, I got mad again."

"You couldn't go anywhere now. What did you do?"

"I observed, and I tried to scare him. I tried to scare away the young girls because I wanted to protect them against him."

"Did you succeed?"

"With a couple of them, yes. They thought working there was scary, and they felt like someone was watching them. Before long, rumour had it the manor was haunted."

"And you were doing the haunting?"

"Yes, that would be me."

"Were there other ghosts at the manor?"

"No."

"How long did you stay at the manor? Was being there enough for you, or what happened next?"

"The way I remember it, I stayed for many years, observing life in the inner circle."

"And you were the lady of the manor now. Was that satisfying?"

"Not really, but it felt satisfying because I was so mad and bitter."

"Did you ever reach a point where you'd had enough?"

"I didn't feel like I'd had enough. I had all the time in the world, but I did decide to branch out a little. I observed other people's lives and patterns, mostly in terms of how much and how men listen to and view their wives."

"So, what brought you to this house where Gitte and Henrik live?"

"I saw this bubbly, playful side of Gitte that Henrik didn't seem to notice, and that made her interesting to me."

"Do they have the same relationship as you and the master? Where she wanted the fairy-tale ending and he wanted the recognition and was more preoccupied with what other people thought, or are they from separate worlds?"

"He's more conservative; she's more creative. There are so many options, if he would just expand his horizon a little bit and look at all the things she has to offer."

Laurens looks at Gitte and asks, "Do you connect with anything Marta's saying?"

"Your story has gone straight to my heart. It brings me a lot of sorrow, and yes, I connect with your story more than I care to admit," Gitte answers.

"Someone has come for you, Marta. Are you ready to leave?" Laurens asks.

"Yes, I'm tired now, and I think I'm ready."

Laurens steps aside to reveal the master. He looks like he's carrying a heavy burden, and he extends his hand to Marta.

"Come on, Marta, we have a lot to talk about. It's about time we get it all out," the master says.

Marta looks at him in disbelief and says, "What do you mean?"

"I'm sorry about the way things worked out, but what else was I to do at that time? But come, let's walk together," the master says.

Marta takes his hand, and they walk out of the room. As they walk, they begin to fade from view.

Laurens looks back at Gitte.

"How do you feel?"

"I realise that I need to really think about how I was raised, my family, and my relationship with Henrik," Gitte answers sorrowfully.

Afterword

Learn More About Ghosts

A lot of people carry the heavy burdens of guilt and shame. Are you one of them?

This book has given you some insight into some of the emotional reasons why ghosts struggle to let go of this world and move on after they die. You've seen that it's more about feelings than about the actual ghosts. Our aim with this book was to humanise these lost souls and show you that there's nothing to be scared of because, at the end of the day, they're not that different from us. We think it's a privilege to be visited by a ghost because it gives you an opportunity to look inwards and face yourself and your feelings.

Do You Have a Ghost in Your Home?

If you find that you have a ghost in your home, it's because the ghost has some sort of connection with someone or something in your home. They'll stay there as long as they see themselves reflected in someone or find something that they recognise – something they didn't have, something they lost, or something they didn't understand when they were alive. That can be anything from grief and hopelessness to powerlessness and the likes. In other words, you have an influence on their presence and their onward journey on this earth. If you change your path, you might change, downplay, or eliminate the connection they have with you and make it easier for them to move on. It might even make it possible for them to leave this world and move on to the afterlife.

What Can You Do to Help the Ghost?

If you want to help a ghost, start by thinking about your relationship with yourself. How do you treat yourself? What do you think about yourself? Do you tend to say and think negative things about yourself, or are you weighed down by heavy feelings that keep you stuck in the past, unable to focus on the present and have hope for the future? Are you the master of spotting your own flaws and focusing on your failures? And do you often find yourself regretting your life choices, specifically in terms of your relationship, education, and career? If you have a tendency to blame yourself for everything, you might often find yourself thinking, 'If only I'd said this or done that.' If that's how you feel, it might be time to address your own emotions. The more room you allow the past to take up, the less room there is for the future.

Why Is It Important to Help the Ghost to Move On?

Although ghosts aren't dangerous, they come with an incredibly heavy energy. This heavy energy will affect you negatively. If your common trait is a feeling of being insufficient, then your own feelings of insufficiency will only be strengthened by the presence of the ghost, and you might find it hard to think positively and let go of the bad situations or experiences in your past. Your home should be your safe space. It should be the place where you can let down your guard and recharge for the day to come, and a ghost makes that difficult. That's why it's important that both you and the ghost find a way to move on.

How Do You Know If You Have Ghosts in Your House / Around You?

One of the most common signs of a ghost is that there's a space in your home where you, your family, or your pets don't want to be. It can be because there's a smell, a sound, a chill, or a feeling that you don't like. You might see or sense something – like a shadow or a gleam. You might also find that your child asks questions like, 'What's the man / woman / dog doing in my room?' Sometimes people feel like they're being watched or like someone is in the house with them, even when they know they're home alone.

Ingram Content Group UK Ltd.
Milton Keynes UK
UKHW021820160523
421860UK00004B/120

9 781398 444386